helping

people

change

helping

coaching with compassion for

people

lifelong learning and growth

change

Richard Boyatzis | Melvin Smith | Ellen Van Oosten

HARVARD BUSINESS REVIEW PRESS

BOSTON, MASSACHUSETTS

The web addresses referenced in this book were live and correct at the time of the book's publication but may be subject to change.

Library of Congress Cataloging-in-Publication Data

Names: Boyatzis, Richard E., author. | Smith, Melvin (Melvin L.), author. |
    Van Oosten, Ellen, author.
Title: Helping people change : coaching with compassion for lifelong learning
    and growth / by Richard E. Boyatzis (PhD), Melvin Smith (PhD), Ellen Van
    Oosten (PhD).
Description: Boston : Harvard Business Review Press, [2019]
Identifiers: LCCN 2019007729 | ISBN 9781633696563 (hardcover)
Subjects: LCSH: Personal coaching. | Mentoring. | Self-actualization
    (Psychology) | Emotional intelligence.
Classification: LCC BF637.P36 B69 2019 | DDC 158.3—dc23
LC record available at https://lccn.loc.gov/2019007729

ISBN: 978-1-63369-656-3
eISBN: 978-1-63369-657-0

The paper used in this publication meets the requirements of the American National Standard for Permanence of Paper for Publications and Documents in Libraries and Archives Z39.48-1992.

To Sandy, Jennifer, and Scott,
our spouses and best coaches

CONTENTS

ACKNOWLEDGMENTS

We deeply appreciate the support and encouragement of our colleagues at the Department of Organizational Behavior at Case Western Reserve University. Specifically, we would like to thank our department chair, Professor Diana Bilimoria, and fellow Professors Diane Bergeron, Susan Case, Corinne Coen, Harlow Cohen, David Cooperrider, Ron Fry, Chris Laszlo, Tracey Messer, and John Paul Stephens. We could not function without the regular and positive support of our department administrator, Lila Robinson, and Patricia Petty, Assistant Director of the MPOD program. Over the years, many doctoral students in Organizational Behavior have participated in our Coaching Study Group, which eventually morphed into the Intentional Change Study Group, namely, Emily Amdurer, Estelle Archibold, Alim Beveridge, Kevin Cavanagh, Gareth Craze, Udayan Dhar, Darren Good, Anita Howard, Jennifer Nash, Angela Passarelli, Brigette Rapisarda, Kylie Rochford, Tiffany Schroeder Kriz, Scott Taylor, Njoke Thomas, Mandy Varley, and Doc Warr. Annie McKee, who was a doctoral student and a member of our study groups in an earlier era, continues to be an inspiration to us and a frequent coauthor with Richard, and a leader of coaching groups as well at the University of Pennsylvania Graduate School of Education's PennCLO Executive Doctoral Program. There have been other doctoral students whose research on personal vision, emotional intelligence, and the quality of relationships was a great help to us. They are Manoj Babu, Jodi Berg, Amanda Blake, Kathleen Buse, Masud Khawaja, Loren Dyck, Linda Pittenger, Joanne Quinn, and John Schaffner.

We are inspired by new ideas, research, and better methods for coaching from our colleagues at the Coaching Research Lab (CRL) at the Weatherhead School of Management, namely Professors Tony Jack, Angela Passarelli, Scott Taylor, and Kylie Rochford, and from our doctoral students who keep CRL and its studies moving ahead, namely Gareth Craze, Kevin Cavanagh, Udayan Dhar, Jessi Hinz, Mercedes McBride-Walker, Mai Trinh, Mandy Varley, and Maria Volkova. We are also indebted to organizational members of the Coaching Research Lab who partner with us to advance research and practice in the field of coaching. We extend a special note of appreciation to Fifth Third Bank and Erie Insurance, whose initial support as founding members of the CRL served as an essential launch pad for the entire initiative. We would also like to thank past and present organizational members, including Crown Equipment, Dealer Tire, Ford, Lubrizol, Moen (Global Plumbing Group), J. M. Smucker Company, Sandia National Laboratories, and Steris.

We would like to acknowledge our dedicated colleagues at Weatherhead Executive Education, who have been long-term allies in our challenge to bring coaching to the world of work. They include Chuck Black, Jennifer Carr, Kim Goldsberry, Mindy Kannard, Aparna Malhotra, Charlene McGrue, Ericka McPherson, Lori Neiswander, Sharon Norris, Jennifer O'Connor-Neskey, Lyndy Rutkowski, Laniece Washington, Laura Weber Smith, Michelle Wilson, our new executive director, Chris Kush, and our former associate dean, Denise Douglas. Last but not least, we could not do this coaching work without the incredibly talented and committed coaches in our Weatherhead Executive Education coaching pool. We are grateful for their continued partnership and service.

Most of the stories in this book come from our decades of teaching in undergraduate, graduate, and executive education programs at Case Western Reserve University's Weatherhead School of Management. While listing each one isn't possible here, we wish to express our deep appreciation to our past and present students for their openness to lifelong learning. Through our conversations both inside and outside of the classroom, you have helped us to refine our theories, models, inquiries, and hunches. You have helped us to learn, grow, and change as educators, presenters, and colleagues.

Colleagues and friends from around the world have been beyond supportive as we developed our approach to coaching and conducting exciting research. Since 2000, from ESADE in Barcelona, this group has included Professors Joan Manuel Batista, Marc Correa, Rob Emmerling, Laura Guillen, Ricard Serlavos, and former doctoral students Basak Conboy, Amy Leverton, Leticia Mosteo, Roy Mouwad, Alaide Sipadas, and Ferran Valesco. Also included are our friends and colleagues at Università Ca´ Foscari in Venice: Professors Fabrizio Gerli, Sara Bonesso, Anna Commacho, and Laura Cortelazzo.

Throughout this book and in the list of publications cited in the endnotes, you will find other colleagues whose coauthorship and ongoing dialogue have helped our research and ideas continue to develop. People who have helped us learn include Kathy Kram, Nancy Blaize, and Terry Maltbia; Carol Kauffman, Margaret Moore, and Susan David, founders of the Institute of Coaching at McLean Hospital, a Harvard Medical School Affiliate; Dan Goleman, who taught Richard to write for normal people and has been a friend and cocreator of ideas and tests since 1969; Annie McKee and Fran Johnston; Cary Cherniss, Poppy McLeod, Vanessa Druskat, and Helen Riess.

We are deeply grateful to the team of editors at Harvard Business Review Press, especially Jeff Kehoe, who believed in this work from his first read of our proposal. We also extend our special thanks to Lucy McCauley for her encouragement and thoughtful and careful attention to this book. Her insightful logic and word magic helped turn our thoughts into gracefully flowing text.

Richard would like to thank his son, Mark Scott, for decades of patience with his distracted father and for coaxing from him a better and clearer writing style. He would also like to thank the Michael Horvitz family for their gracious support of his endowed chair, which has provided the much-needed support for all of the fMRI and many of the studies we have conducted and continue to conduct on coaching.

Above all, Richard would like to acknowledge and thank Professor David A. Kolb for his mentorship, guidance, friendship, and colleagueship over fifty-three years. Professor Kolb brought Richard into the field of psychology from aeronautics and astronautics, inspired him, and helped him find a path beginning in 1967 with a series of research studies on helping that continues to have an impact today. Professor Kolb guided Richard toward the PhD program in psychology at Harvard and introduced him to others who became mentors and friends, such as Professor David McClelland, Professor Edgar Schein, Dave Berlew, Fritz Steele, Professor Bob Rosenthal, Professor Robert Freed Bales, and many others. This book and the research behind it truly began in the spring of 1967 with the first empirical study on helping and then a book on helping that did not get published. But the ideas and passion remained.

Melvin would like to thank his immediate and extended family, most notably his mother, Mary, and his late father, Melvin Sr., who provided him with a loving home full of joy, compassion, support, and encouragement that always made him feel confident in pursuing his dreams; his wife of thirty-one years, Jennifer, a loving partner who makes him a better person and with whom he has built a wonderful and more fulfilling life than he ever imagined; and their two sons, Ryan and Evan, who serve not only as a consistent source of pride in all that they do, but also as a source of awe and wonder as they continue to grow into impressive young men, carving out their own unique life paths.

Ellen would like to thank her family for encouraging her to experience what it means to help others and to be helped in loving, meaningful ways. She would like to honor her mother, Mary Ellen Brooks, and her late father, Thomas Brooks, for being her first coaches and for showing her what unconditional love and sacrifice really mean. She would like to thank her husband, Scott, for his generous spirit, for the compassion he extends to her and to everyone around him, and for his ability to keep her laughing through life's inevitable ups and downs. She would also like to thank their children, Maureen and Thomas, who keep her grounded and bring joy to her life with their curious, strong minds and open, loving hearts. She would also like to thank her extended family and friends for their gifts of support in all its forms.

Finally, Melvin and Ellen would like to thank Richard, who has been not only an inspiring coauthor and colleague, but also an incredible mentor and friend. He has served as a model of how meaningful and joyful a life of helping people change can be!

Richard Boyatzis   Melvin Smith
Richard.Boyatzis@case.edu   Melvin.Smith@case.edu

Ellen Van Oosten
Ellen.VanOosten@case.edu

helping

people

change

the heart of helping

how to really help others learn and grow

After tying off the final sutures, Greg Lakin thanked the operating room staff for another job well done. He removed his surgical mask and felt pleased that the procedure had gone well. Yet at the same time, he noticed that the joy he used to experience in his work as a plastic surgeon just wasn't there. He wondered: *When—and how—did I lose that excitement?*

He decided to get some help from a coach. An overachiever since childhood, Greg had attained one success after another on the road to becoming a surgeon. When he began working with a coach, he shared that this drive for success was partially fueled by the feeling that he needed to constantly prove himself. In the process, however, Greg had lost sight of his true passions and life aspirations. For instance, he wished to have a more balanced life with time for travel and getting back to his running. He also expressed a desire to get back to South Florida, where he had grown up, so he could be closer to his family and childhood friends. Yet his current path had him working seventy to eighty hours a week, leaving little time for the other things he cared about.

Picking up on these things, Greg's coach asked him to spend time reflecting on and articulating the details of his personal vision—and to try to separate his heartfelt desires from the *shoulds* and *oughts* in his life. As he gave himself permission to do that, a light switched on. Greg discovered what he really wanted, and he experienced the positive energy and motivation that comes from such clarity. Working closely with his coach, Greg began to change his life in ways he couldn't have imagined just a few months before. We'll look at Greg's story in depth in chapter 2, but for now we will say that his life, both personally and professionally, has changed for the better in significantly meaningful ways.

how to really help others

Because Greg decided to fully explore his *personal vision* and then actively pursue it, he eventually achieved the work-life balance and closeness with family and friends he desired. And he rediscovered joy in his life. When it comes to coaching other people, our research shows that excavating and articulating an individual's personal vision is crucial. More than resolving immediate problems and more than trying to help someone achieve a set of prescribed goals or meet certain standards, uncovering a person's hopes and dreams is the key that unlocks positive emotions and intrinsic motivation—and propels that person to genuine, lasting change.

But guiding others to achieve their hearts' desires isn't just for coaches. Everywhere you look, you see examples of people helping other people to learn or change. In fact, when asked about the people who influenced us most in life, many of us think first about our parents, athletic coaches, or teachers—perhaps a teacher like Kyle Schwartz.

When Kyle began teaching third grade, she suspected there was more to know about her students than what their enrollment data forms or their standardized test scores revealed. To be a truly effective teacher, she decided, she'd somehow have to learn what her students were thinking about—what mattered to *them*.[1] She asked them to complete the following sentence: "I wish my teacher knew . . ."

Here's what Kyle learned:

> "I wish my teacher knew my reading log is not signed because my mom is not around a lot."
>
> "I wish my teacher knew I love animals and I would do anything for animals. I would love to work at the MSPCA so I could help animals get adopted."
>
> "I wish my teacher knew that my family and I live in a shelter."[2]

The list goes on, each answer more moving and revealing than the last. To say the least, the students' words triggered Kyle's compassion. Even more, they gave her the information she needed to help them as their teacher. Now she knew what mattered most to the kids—and it had little to do with the standard daily lesson plans found in third-grade classrooms.

Kyle's question to her students has gone viral on the Twitter-sphere, and it's making its way into primary-school classrooms around the world. Clearly, people are hungry to find effective ways to understand and help other people. Her question is simple, yet it isn't often asked by people who presumably want to help others. As teachers, managers, colleagues, parents, and coaches of all kinds, we become preoccupied with our tasks and agendas and forget to ask such basic, revealing questions—questions that will tell us something important about the people we want to help. Or perhaps we don't ask such questions because we're afraid of the answers and what issues and emotions might surface. It's sometimes easier to ignore or deny them, to stay closed off to our awareness or sensitivity to another person. We simply proceed, undeterred by people's needs and wishes outside the scope of our schedule or lesson plan.

And yet, as Greg Lakin's story illustrated, those "distractions"—people's hurts and sorrows, their dreams and most heartfelt wishes—nevertheless remain. They still affect our students, clients, patients, subordinates, peers, and children on the deepest levels, the level on which true learning and change occurs. In response to her question, the students in Kyle Schwartz's classroom told her not only what was troubling them; they also told her their aspirations and visions for themselves.

As we see it, that is how Kyle tapped into the possibility of growth and transformation for those children. Rather than placing the focus on *herself* as the teacher and what she needed to teach her third-graders, she focused on the students, the *learners*. This enabled her to build better and more meaningful relationships with and among the students. She was able to build a community with a common or shared purpose of listening and caring for each other.

The two stories we've just shared emerged from very different contexts. But they are both about helping others to learn, grow, and change, and that is the focus of this book. The fact is that everyone needs help, not only third-grade children and not only surgeons at an impasse in their careers. We all need help to make important changes in our lives and work and to learn new things.

This book will show you how to help others more effectively. Note that, although our focus as authors, researchers, and educators happens to be on the coaching profession (executive, career, life, team and peer coaching), we intend this book for many different audiences. That is, anyone who wishes to help people—managers, mentors, counselors, therapists, clerics, teachers, parents, athletic coaches, colleagues, friends—will find an important guide here, including a number of practical exercises to develop your helping skills.

Specifically, we'll describe in this book what our research has shown helps people most profoundly and sustainably. That is, as Greg Lakin and Kyle Schwartz learned, the best way to help other people to learn, grow, and change is by helping them move closer to their ideal self—their dreams and vision of their ideal future.

coaching with compassion

We've based this book on the premise that, when done effectively, coaching and helping of all kinds create three specific changes in people seeking help. First, they will find or reaffirm and articulate their personal vision, including dreams, passion, purpose, and values. Second, they will experience changes in behavior, thoughts, and/or feelings that will move them closer to realizing their personal vision. And third, they will build or maintain what we call a *resonant relationship* with the coach or helper and ideally with other supportive people in their lives.

But how do we get there? How do we go from having a good intention to help someone to actually fulfilling the promise of the three kinds of changes we've just named? It isn't always an intuitive or obvious process. Often, when we try to help people, we focus on correcting a problem. After all, we are often more experienced and can see what the person *should do* to lead a better life, be more productive, or learn more. We know what is good for them. Or we see ourselves in the person or situation, and we project what we once did, or would do, onto the other person. Sometimes people come to us seeking a solution to a problem. As helpers, we hear those people asking for symptom relief, so we work with them on something far short of their deeper desires and needs.

That is a mistake. In our attempt to coach a person seeking help, most of us naturally take a problem-centered approach, focusing on the gaps between where they are and where we think they should or could be. We are trying to *fix* them. This does not work well, if at all, to motivate sustained learning, change, or adaptation. It might, at times, lead to quick corrective action. But when people do respond, they often do so out of a sense of obligation and lack the inner motivation needed to manifest the change they desire. Or they feel the need to do something, even if it is not a sustainable solution. *That* is the key: Is the effort sustainable? Will it last? Does the person have the deep commitment needed to continue the effort toward change or learning?

Of course, there are times when people have some serious problems they must resolve. But our research tells us that when the context is a gap or a shortfall that needs addressing, the energy and effort needed to sustain change is typically absent. Conversely, when the context is a long-term dream or vision, people draw energy from that vision and are able to sustain their effort to change, even through difficult times.

When a coach or other type of helper is able to craft such a context, we call this *coaching with compassion*—that is, coaching with a genuine sense of caring and concern, focusing on the other person, providing support and encouragement, and facilitating the discovery and pursuit of that person's dreams and passions. That is what Kyle Schwartz did when she reached out to her students and asked what they wanted to *tell her*. In this book, we contrast that approach with what we describe as *coaching for compliance*—where, rather than helping someone articulate and fulfill a desired future, the coach attempts to facilitate the person's movement toward some externally defined objective. Today, coaching for compliance is the default approach in many kinds of helping, from athletic coaching to teaching to parenting to the doctor-patient relationship. This is especially the case in business coaching and all too often for executive coaching, where a coach is hired explicitly to guide the executive or employee to meet specific criteria for success within the organization.

In certain situations, coaching for compliance can be effective in helping someone achieve a very specific and predetermined goal, such as earning a promotion to a certain role. But our research shows such coaching rarely leads to sustained change in individuals, nor does it help them strive toward their full potential, let alone achieve it. Coaching with compassion, on the other hand, does just that. It helps people discover the ways that they would most like to grow and change in their lives and provides them with a process and support to make and sustain those changes. One of our students put it this way: "All those that were important figures in my life planted seeds of inspiration and ideas and then allowed me the freedom to take that in directions that worked best for me, all the while supporting and encouraging my choices."

We contend that this is what great coaches do. Great coaches and the best teachers, managers, colleagues, and friends engage us in conversations that inspire us. They make us want to grow, develop, and change in meaningful ways, and they help us to do so. They help us pursue a personal vision rather than merely to dutifully fulfill a life of *shoulds* and *oughts*.

the research: why coaching with compassion works

To make changes stick, our research shows that it has to be intentional and internally motivated rather than imposed from the outside. That's why coaching with compassion starts with a person articulating his *ideal self* or vision for himself—as Greg Lakin did when he realized he wanted a more balanced life, connected with his family and old friends. This anchored Greg, both psychologically and emotionally, in what we call a *positive emotional attractor* (PEA) that opened him up to possibilities and the excitement that can come with change. In the chapters to come, we will contrast the PEA with the negative emotional attractor (NEA)—usually triggered by *shoulds* or outside mandates—and show how the one helps and the other inhibits the process of lasting change.

Nevertheless, both the PEA and NEA are needed for growth—it's just a matter of getting the "dosage" and sequence right in order to be effective rather than inhibiting. In this book, we also will explain how the PEA acts as a tipping point that helps a person move from one step to another in an important developmental process guided by *Intentional Change Theory* (ICT), which we will explain in chapter 3. We will also share here many other findings from our research. We'll talk about how the coaching process should always begin with an individual's personal vision, and how the coaching process itself needs to be holistic, encompassing the individual's life as a whole—not just a few discrete aspects.

An important note: We believe that in order for coaches or anyone to help another person, they must first feel inspired. Without recognizing our own motivations and feelings, we can do little to truly connect with another person in a helpful way. That is, coaches—be they teachers, parents, doctors, nurses, clerics, or professional executive coaches—should understand their own emotions and develop a personal vision. That is the basis for an authentic relationship between the helper and person being helped or coached. Therefore, we intend the exercises included throughout this book not only for the coachee but also for the coach.

Everything we are writing about is based on in-depth research that we have conducted personally—individually and as a team— over the past fifty years. That is part of what sets this book apart from many other books on helping, management, leadership or coaching: it is based on evidence. The research began in 1967, with studies on how adults helped each other develop or didn't. Longitudinal research (i.e., tracking people over time) about behavior change in arenas from management to addiction was completed in companies, government agencies, nonprofits, graduate school programs, and hospitals around the world. This research was followed by almost twenty years of hormonal and neuroimaging studies. We cite our own research as well as studies completed by our doctoral students and those of colleagues. In addition, we are each coaches and educators, so our stories draw on our own personal and professional coaching experiences.

As researchers and authors, the three of us work closely together at Case Western University, and we teach together in our Coach Certificate Program at the Weatherhead School of Management. Moreover, together we have launched several coaching initiatives. The Coaching Research Lab (CRL) was formed in 2014. The CRL brings together scholars and practitioners to advance coaching research. Our massive, open, online course (MOOC), "Conversations That Inspire: Coaching Learning, Leadership, and Change," was started in 2015. The course focuses on a compassion-based approach to coaching and has attracted more than 140,000 participants. An earlier MOOC on inspiring leadership through emotional intelligence that introduced many of these ideas has attracted more than 800,000 participants from more than 215 countries.

Our studies make the case clearly—specifically, the behavioral, hormonal, and neuroimaging studies show the differential impact of coaching others around their dreams and vision (coaching with compassion) versus coaching them around some externally defined objective (coaching for compliance). Further, we've seen in our own students how effective coaching with compassion can be. Such coaching, in conjunction with a four-month-long leadership development course, has resulted in significant improvements, as observed by others, in the emotional and social intelligence competencies the students chose to develop to support their personal visions. Together, these provide a sound, scientific foundation for the development of *how* to effectively coach and help others manifest sustained, desired change.

a guide to this book

As you read this book, you'll delve further into each of the topics explored in this introductory chapter, gleaning insight and practical skills along the way to help you most effectively coach or help others in most contexts. Throughout the book, we highlight specific takeaways (*key learning points*), relevant research studies (*research spotlights*), and provide references and more detail in the endnotes. For the practical reader, we offer specific, time-tested exercises at the end of most chapters (*reflection and application exercises*). We want to promote reflection as active and emotional learning, not just knowledge. We also provide conversation guides at the end of most chapters, which include questions about these topics to mull over with friends and colleagues. The benefits of the book come in part from personally reflecting on the ideas and techniques and, as our neuroimaging studies have shown, talking about these reflections and experiences with others. Discussing ideas with others is what makes them come alive in a more accessible way. The conversation guides are a useful way to make that happen. Although we hope we've written this book in such a way that you'll enjoy reading it from cover to cover, you can also use it as a reference guide by going straight to certain chapters or to the key learning points, exercises, and the other items highlighted throughout.

Briefly, the book unfolds as follows: Chapter 2 explores the uses and definitions of coaching and other ways that people help one another. As the examples we offer from real coaching cases illustrate, at the heart of any such helping process is a set of experiences within the relationship between the person being helped and the helper. Chapter 3 delves more deeply into how to coach with compassion versus coaching for compliance. Our approach begins with the realization that people can change when they want to change. We then describe the five discoveries in Intentional Change Theory as the model of sustained, desired change.

In chapter 4, we discuss what we've learned from recent brain science studies that can enable us to help others more sustainably. Specifically, we focus on how to arouse positive versus negative emotional attractors (PEA and NEA, respectively) in our brains to create a more receptive and motivated emotional state. Chapter 5 takes a deeper dive into the science of PEA and NEA, illustrating that while we need the negative emotional attractor to survive, it is the positive emotional attractor that allows people to thrive and flourish. We discuss how to effectively invoke the positive and create the proper balance between it and the negative, thereby initiating growth and change that lasts.

In chapter 6, we explore the personal vision in depth. Our research shows that discovery and development of such a vision is the neurologically and emotionally most powerful way to engage the positive emotional attractor. A person's vision is her image of a possible future. It is neither goals nor strategy. It is not a forecast of what is likely. It is a dream!

With chapter 7, we begin to focus on how to build resonant relationships and learn to ask the right questions of one another—while listening to the answers—to evoke learning and change.

Both style and timing of questions can inspire the PEA and change, or the opposite. Missing key moments and getting questions out of sequence can turn a possibly motivating conversation into a guilt-inducing grilling. Chapter 8 explores how organizations can foster a culture of coaching by changing company norms, for example: (1) encouraging peer coaching; (2) using external and internal professional coaches; and (3) developing managers to be coaches for their units as well as other areas.

In chapter 9, we illustrate how to take advantage of moments in which a person is ready to be helped, what we call *coachable moments*, and we provide a practical guide for creating a safe space for reflection and openness. The chapter also examines some typical "tough" cases in coaching and demonstrates how the techniques of coaching with compassion can help. Finally, with chapter 10, we end the book with an inspirational appeal, returning you to an exercise first offered in chapter 2, in which we asked you to reflect on who helped you become who you are. After reading the book and learning ways to help others develop, we ask, "Whose list will *you* be on?" After all, connecting with others as they pursue their dreams can be the greatest and most enduring gift in life. It is our legacy!

a message of hope

With this book, then, we present a message of hope. The way to engage and inspire people to learn and change in sustained ways is not difficult, although it may seem counterintuitive at times. We discuss how to stimulate a person to explore new ideas in the context of his dreams and personal vision while on the way to solving specific problems. We will explore what effective coaches and helpers do to help individuals make sustained, desired change in their lives. We will examine not only an approach for effective helping and coaching, but also what it looks like and, perhaps more importantly, what it *feels* like to be engaged in a meaningful coaching relationship from the perspective of both the coach and the person being coached. That's why we use the word *coach* in this book as an approach and a way of *being* more than a title one holds or role that one fulfills.

We believe the ideas and practices in this book will help change the way coaches, leaders, managers, counselors, therapists, teachers, parents, clerics, doctors, nurses, dentists, social workers, and others approach conversations with their clients or patients or students. What's more, we want to inspire more research about coaching and helping. We want to encourage tweaking or modification of the hundreds of coach and manager training programs, medical and nursing education, and any other program aimed at developing individuals in the helping professions to teach a different way to inspire learning and change.

Perhaps most of all, in these recent times of polarized conversation in so many areas of our lives, we want to help people develop the skills to listen with empathy to one another. We want people to be open to learn from one another. We hope we can help people expand their focus outside of themselves and be open to new ideas. By focusing on others and truly helping them, we can build toward a better future in our families, teams, organizations, and communities. With this book, we offer a way to tap into people's desires to learn and change, to motivate themselves and others, and to lead in more compassionate ways.

So let us begin.

conversations that inspire

discovering what is most important

Emily Sinclair was the youngest of three daughters in a family of great soccer players. Her mother played soccer in high school and college, as did her two older sisters. Following in their footsteps, Emily began her freshman year of high school as a standout player on the soccer team. Soon, however, Emily's coach noticed that while she had great skills, she just didn't show the kind of passion for the game he had seen in other star players he'd coached over the years. He noticed something else about Emily: she had an unusually graceful stride as she ran up and down the field. And to his surprise, she seemed to absolutely love the running drills that the other girls dreaded during practice.

One day, acting on a hunch, the coach called Emily over after practice. "Emily, why do you play soccer?" he asked.

Somewhat puzzled, she responded, "Because everyone in my family plays soccer. And because I'm really good at it."

Then the coach asked, "But do you love it?" He could see the wheels spinning in her head as she processed his question.

With a somewhat dejected look, she shook her head. "No. I don't," she answered. "Playing soccer was really fun when I was younger. But now it feels like something I *have* to do. Everyone expects me to be like my mom and sisters. I don't want to let them down."

That's when he realized that his job as Emily's coach had, in an important way, just begun. Rather than continue to try to get her to fit in as a soccer player, he asked about her true interests. He wasn't surprised to learn that she had a passion for running. Running was effortless for her, she said. When running long distances, she felt relaxed and free from all the worries and cares in her life. After several more conversations with Emily and then an initially difficult discussion with her family, the coach and her family gave Emily their blessing to leave the soccer team and switch to running track for the spring semester. By her junior year, Emily was the number one runner on the girls' cross-country team, and as a senior, she led the team to the state finals.

While he lost one of his better players, the coach knew he'd done the right thing by following up on his initial hunch about Emily. In the process, he helped her find her true passion.

This is what great coaches do. It's what great managers do and great teachers do and what others do who know how to help people find and do what they love. They engage us in conversations that inspire us. They make us want to develop and change, and they help us to do so. In this chapter, we will explore how to help people by inspiring them to grow and change. We call this *coaching with compassion*. Its objective? To establish a *resonant relationship* between the coach and the person being coached, which is crucial to creating sustained transformation. Additionally, in this chapter and throughout the book, we will ask you—as someone who wishes to help others—to learn about yourself, your emotions, and motivations. This is a critical step that everyone needs to take before attempting to help others change, and we provide an exercise in this chapter to help you begin that process.

But first, let's define what we mean by *coaching*.

what is coaching?

In this book, we will talk about coaching effectively both as a profession (executive coaches and the like) and as part of our daily lives and roles as managers, teachers, doctors, clerics, parents, friends. Our definition, like most, converges on coaching as a "facilitative or helping relationship with the purpose of achieving some type of change, learning, or new level of individual or organizational performance."[1] An alternative and useful definition comes from the International Coaching Federation (ICF): "Coaching is partnering with an individual or group in a thought-provoking and creative process that inspires them to maximize their personal and professional potential."[2]

Unlike mentoring, which can sometimes last over decades, coaching typically involves a shorter time period and a more specific focus. In our work, we focus on an explicit *dyadic* coaching process, which means that there is a mutual agreement—formal or informal—between coach and coachee that they are participating in a developmental process. Sometimes coaching takes place during predetermined coaching sessions, but it also can occur while walking to or from meetings, at lunch, or in other less formal settings. Note that although the number of professionals using the actual title of "coach" is growing at dramatic rates worldwide, coaching as we use the word also might be an informal or formal advisor, a boss, or a peer.[3]

the coaching conversation

Coaching, when it is most effective, is essentially about helping another person change, learn, or grow in some way. It is about helping people figure out what might be possible or desired in their lives and then helping them figure out how to achieve it.

Like Emily Sinclair, most of us have had someone in our lives who talked to us about our future or otherwise influenced us positively. In our graduate courses, executive education programs, and in our "Conversations That Inspire" MOOC, we ask participants

people who have helped me the most

"The people who have most helped me to grow as a person believed in my potential and inspired my creativity and desire to learn. They have challenged me, and when I have accepted the challenge, the results surprised even myself. Another common pattern in their behavior was their genuine care for my well-being and their emotional involvement in my success."
   —Stanley (Canada)

"These people not only see the spark, but they nurture it. They help bring out your best by allowing you to flourish. Feeling my 'spark' acknowledged also made me feel affirmed in a way I hadn't experienced before."
   —Angela (USA)

"All those that were important figures in my life planted seeds of inspiration and ideas, and then allowed me the freedom to take that in directions that worked best for me, all the while supporting, and encouraging my choices. That gave me huge confidence."
   —Beverly (USA)

to recall the people who really helped them most in their lives. One person referred to her blind step-grandfather, who loved her unconditionally and instilled within her a passion for learning. For another individual, it was a friend who made him feel accepted— no matter what issue he was struggling with or what outrageous goal he had in mind. He always knew he wasn't being judged but rather encouraged and fully supported.

Many participants referred to individuals who actively listened to them. They spoke of coaches or others who asked reflective questions that helped them analyze and delve deeper into their thought process and who—through their care, concern, and insight—helped

"They valued me as a person in a way I had never seen myself, thus unleashing completely new thinking, opportunities, and possibilities, which led to lots of energy, and me driving for new changes which I would never have pursued without this input."
—Arjun (India)

"These persons believed in me, did not judge me, and showed compassion. They did not refrain from telling me things I would not like to hear, but I always felt respected. Another common pattern is that they did not want to impose their opinion on me. To the contrary, they encouraged me to find the answers I needed in myself."
—Kwabena (Ghana)

"I think the single most important pattern that became clear in all these people was that they inspired me to do something—they didn't just instruct me as to what I should be doing."
—Malcolm (United Kingdom)

them work through confusing emotions. Often these helpers guided them to develop a realistic plan of action, all while helping them feel understood and supported in just the right way.

Managers in other courses, training programs, and MOOCs described individuals who motivated and inspired them to pursue their dreams and to ultimately achieve more than they ever thought was possible. They wrote about people who helped them grow by focusing on their strengths and instilling within them a sense of confidence and capability. They also described individuals who weren't afraid to give them honest feedback, even when it was difficult to hear. In those cases, however, the feedback (when effective) was given with kindness and compassion, in a spirit meant to build them up rather than tear them down. (For more specific quotes from MOOC participants, see the sidebar "People Who Have Helped Me the Most.")

A number of pertinent themes emerge from these statements. People who influence others most often (1) serve as a source of inspiration, (2) show a genuine sense of caring and concern, (3) provide support and encouragement, and (4) facilitate the discovery and pursuit of the dreams and passions of the people they are coaching/trying to help. Collectively, these behaviors represent what we call *coaching with compassion*, which we introduced in chapter 1 and will discuss in greater detail in chapter 3. We contrast this approach with what can be described as *coaching for compliance*, where the coach attempts to facilitate the person's movement toward some externally defined objective (rather than helping them articulate and fulfill their desired future). While common, coaching for compliance rarely leads to sustained change in individuals being coached, and rarely does it result in them striving for, let alone achieving, their full potential. Coaching with compassion, on the other hand, does just that. It helps individuals discover the ways in which they would most like to grow and change in their lives, and it provides them with a process and facilitative support to make and sustain those changes.

We have documented evidence of the effectiveness of coaching with compassion through longitudinal studies conducted with both MBA students and professional fellows at Case Western Reserve University. When the graduate students were matched with a coach trained in coaching with compassion as a key part of a semester-long leadership development course, they saw dramatic and significant improvements in the emotional and social intelligence competencies (i.e., behavior as seen by others) that they chose to develop in support of their personal vision. (See the research spotlight below for additional details on these studies.)[4] To be specific, coaching with compassion in this context is working with people to build compelling personal visions, assess themselves through 360-degree and other feedback, develop a learning plan, and engage in peer coaching to practice new behaviors (more of this will become clear in the chapters that follow).

research spotlight

Richard Boyatzis, working over a number of years with different colleagues, conducted thirty-nine longitudinal studies appearing in sixteen peer-reviewed articles and book chapters.[5] The studies followed a graduate course based on coaching with compassion, along with Intentional Change Theory (which we will explore in detail in chapter 3). The findings showed that emotional and social intelligence (ESI) competencies can be developed dramatically in adults (twenty-five- to thirty-five-year-old MBAs, as well as professional fellows averaging forty-nine years old) and that the improvement lasts from five to seven years. Specifically, the findings showed an increase of 61 percent of ESI over one to two years after entry into the MBA program for full-time students. Part-time MBAs improved slightly less at 54 percent at three to five years after taking the course. Two of the part-time MBA cohorts showed sustained improvement of 54 percent two years after graduation, which was five to seven years after entry into the program and taking the course. This is in contrast to outcome studies of eight above-average MBA programs showing about a 2 percent improvement over one to two years (which we suspect would drop over time) and corporate and government training programs showing an improvement of 11 percent that occurred three to eighteen months after training (which again, we suspect would drop considerably over time).[6]

rediscovering lost joy

Recall our story of Greg Lakin, the plastic surgeon, from chapter 1. When he realized he was unhappy, he turned to a coach who was able to offer him unconditional support throughout his process of growth and change. Many of us experience times in life when we feel a sense of being disconnected from who we really are. At one such moment, Greg turned to get some help—in his case, from a coach who was provided as part of a larger leadership development program.

It wasn't always easy. After all, Greg had been pursuing a successful career, having attained at an early age the positions of Chief of Plastic and Reconstructive Surgery, and Director of the Craniofacial Center at University Hospital's Rainbow Babies & Children's Hospital in Cleveland, Ohio. As Greg began to work with his coach, he realized that these accomplishments were part of a trajectory, begun in childhood, of an insatiable desire to achieve. Not only had he attended a leading national Ivy League prep school where he'd been a standout varsity athlete in three sports, he was also recognized as one of the top students academically. His drive for success continued through his undergraduate experience at Duke University, then medical school abroad, followed by plastic surgery residency, and ultimately fellowships in craniofacial research at the University of Pennsylvania and craniofacial surgery at UCLA.

Yet the joy of achievement had long since vanished for Greg. Through in-depth conversations with his coach, he started to uncover his most heartfelt dreams and visions for his life. He came to understand that in his focus to become "successful," he'd lost sight of his true passions and life aspirations—things like running and living close to family and friends where he'd grown up, in South Florida. How would he ever find time to pursue these things, when his current job had him working seventy to eighty hours a week?

Greg's coach asked him to spend some time reflecting on and further articulating and exploring the various aspects of his personal vision—and to try to separate his wants and his true desires from the *shoulds* and *oughts* in his life. Soon Greg began to achieve greater clarity, which restored his positive energy and motivation. He followed up on a lead he'd been given regarding a full-service dermatology and plastic surgery practice in his home town of Fort Lauderdale, Florida, that was looking to add another plastic surgeon. Although he hadn't even been considering a new job, Greg quickly realized that this was the ideal position for him. In time, he joined a successful practice that would take him back to his hometown, where he'd be surrounded by family and close childhood friends. But rather than having to work seventy- to eighty-hour weeks as he'd been doing for years, Greg would be operating only one day a week—and at a significant increase in compensation.

Finally, Greg would have the balance he'd sought. It didn't happen overnight, but it was still a much faster and more satisfying process than he'd believed possible. As he shared with his coach, he said, "I must be dreaming. I've been offered what appears to be my ideal job, making significantly more money while working fewer hours, in my beautiful hometown of Fort Lauderdale. How could it get any better than this?"

resonance and the coaching relationship

Had Greg's coach been focused on coaching him for compliance to some external standard, she might have steered him toward finding ways to work more efficiently in order to reduce his hours. Or, she might have worked with Greg on how to most effectively position himself for his next promotion at the hospital. Lucky for Greg, however, his coach understood how to coach with compassion and help him identify and move toward his *ideal self*—his deepest hopes and dreams. In so doing, the two developed a *resonant relationship*—one built on positive emotion and genuine connection. That relationship would ultimately help Greg create change that would be holistic and sustainable, rather than change-focused on solving a particular problem.

By helping individuals identify and pursue their dreams, truly effective coaches and other helpers build and maintain resonant relationships with the people they coach. These relationships are characterized by (1) an overall positive emotional tone and (2) a genuine, authentic connection with the person being coached. There is a sense of flow in the relationship, with the coach being in tune with the person she is intending to help.

In their 2005 book *Resonant Leadership*, Richard Boyatzis and Annie McKee discussed those two elements as *pathways to renewal*. They suggested that when leaders experience mindfulness, hope, and compassion, it can help them recover from the effects of the chronic stress associated with serving in a leadership role. As it turns out, these pathways to renewal also serve as pathways to the creation of engaging coaching relationships. When a resonant relationship is created, the coach and the person being coached become attuned as they operate on the same emotional wavelength. The stress-reducing and life-enhancing benefits of mindfulness, hope, and compassion flow seamlessly between the two in a symbiotic fashion. Such was the case with Claire Scott Miller and Neil Thompson.

the power of meaningful connections

Just as her plane was about to touch down at London's Heathrow Airport, Claire Scott Miller felt an anxious excitement. She would soon meet for the first time face-to-face with an executive with whom she'd developed a rewarding coaching relationship over the past three years, all via phone conversations.

When she'd begun coaching Neil Thompson, he was Director of Strategic Business Development for a Scotland-based global leader in integrated fluid transfer and power and control solutions for industries such as oil and gas, renewable energy, original equipment manufacturers, marine, and defense. Claire had been retained to help Neil reach the C-suite. From the beginning, she took extra care to make a meaningful connection. This entailed going beyond achieving an understanding of Neil's professional goals and objectives. She also explored the dreams and aspirations he had for his family and his life outside of work. After experiencing positive results from his coaching relationship with Claire, Neil requested a one-year extension at the conclusion of the initial coaching contract, and the following year he did the same. By the time Neil was promoted to Chief Commercial Officer, Claire had clearly become a trusted supporter, helping to facilitate his ongoing pursuit of his personal and professional aspirations.

And now, because of the quality of the relationship Claire had established, she was about to meet Neil in person. After visiting family in London, she and her husband traveled to Edinburgh to attend the Edinburgh International Festival and Royal Military Tattoo. Neil was vacationing in Glasgow that week, but took time out of his vacation to travel with his family (including a six-month-old baby) to Edinburgh to spend some time with Claire and her family. While this was their first time meeting in person, the conversation was comfortable and free-flowing, almost like spending time with longtime good friends.

Clearly, her work as a coach had succeeded. She'd sought to establish a resonant relationship with Neil and to help him articulate and pursue his dreams. In the process, she had built a quality relationship based on genuine care and concern—essential elements of coaching with compassion. She did this by asking Neil meaningful questions and attentively connecting with him around his responses. But she was also willing to engage in a certain degree of self-disclosure, occasionally sharing things about herself in the service of Neil's development and their coaching relationship. Claire's sharing and her willingness to demonstrate vulnerability also served as a model for Neil, making him more comfortable openly sharing things that became useful in his development.[7]

The kind of resonant relationship that Claire established while coaching Neil typically involves at least three elements: (1) the experience of mindfulness, (2) the arousal of hope, and (3) the demonstration of compassion.

When coaches are mindful, they are fully present with the person they are coaching, staying in the moment with full and conscious awareness. They are completely tuned into that person and what they are saying, as well as what they seem to be feeling. Coaches who are mindful are also very self-aware, understanding what they are personally thinking and feeling at any given moment and being careful not to project their own thoughts and feelings onto the person they are coaching. This leads to a genuine and authentic connection where the person being coached often feels as if he is having a comfortable and relaxed conversation with a close friend.

Great coaches also ignite a deep sense of meaning and hope. Sometimes they are reigniting what the person they are coaching once felt but has lost over time. For people to become their ideal future selves, they have to understand what gives them meaning and purpose in life and feel hopeful that it's possible to achieve. Thus an effective coach poses questions that invite reflection and uncover what is most important and meaningful to the individual. Even with a deep sense of meaning and purpose, however, people rarely can move forward unless they also feel hope. Effective coaches therefore help create that sense of hope, instilling a sense of confidence in the people they coach that the ideal future they envision is indeed achievable with intentional, focused effort.

Finally, effective coaches demonstrate their care for others. This goes beyond a general sense of empathy or a simple understanding of what the person is feeling. Instead, such coaches care deeply and are willing to act on that concern, offering guidance and support as necessary to help the individuals they are coaching achieve their dreams. Again, this is the essence of coaching with compassion.

Ultimately, effective coaches inspire others. After a coaching conversation, people should feel charged up, excited, and full of purposeful movement toward their dreams. But it isn't only the people being coached who will feel charged up. Effective coaches, too, will leave the conversations feeling inspired.

This phenomenon, called *emotional contagion*, is a tacit exchange that can occur between people in under a second, in certain situations. It occurs on many levels, including at the neural network level. We will explain this phenomenon in more detail in chapter 4, but for now, we'll say that emotional contagion allows the coach and the person she is coaching to literally affect and infect each other with feelings of hope, compassion, mindfulness, and exciting possibilities in life and work.[8]

who helped you?

Earlier in this chapter, we shared some of the responses from participants in our MOOC. Now it's your turn. Regardless of the specific relationship, many of us can recall conversations where someone inspired us to figure out what we cared about or really wanted to do with our life—conversations that sparked deep reflections and ultimately led us to take actions that shaped our future.

As we pointed out in chapter 1, doing the exercises in this book is important for you as someone who wishes to help others. It is key to helping you learn how to identify your own motivations, emotions, and aspirations—and therefore create resonant relationships with the people you wish to help. Conducting these exercises should help ignite a flame inside of you around your passions and dreams of an ideal future. That internal flame should create a positive emotional experience. And as you coach others, it will be like touching a match to kindling—such is the contagious nature of emotions.

So, think of a time in your life when someone coached you in a way that really made you think, a time when someone sparked that flame inside of you around your passion and it changed the trajectory of your life. Maybe it was an athletic coach, or a high-school teacher, a parent or other relative, or a manager or mentor at work. Maybe it was a close personal friend. Think about how they made you feel—Hopeful? Motivated? Full of ideas and possibilities? Most likely they also showed genuine care and concern for you. Perhaps they helped you realize and appreciate who you are when you are at your best. They may have helped you envision a future for yourself that was exciting and energizing. They also probably offered their unconditional support to help you achieve whatever it was you wished.

It's important to distinguish those people who helped you from others who perhaps *tried* to help you but somehow fell short of the mark. Far from filling you with hope, those people left you feeling discouraged, inadequate, or forced into a box of their making—not yours.

Now complete the reflection and application exercise at the end of this chapter. Later in the book, we will return to it.

———————

In chapter 3, we will look more deeply at how to coach with compassion (versus compliance), and we will explore the five discoveries of

Intentional Change Theory (ICT)—critical for making sustained, desired change.

key learning points

1. Great coaches inspire, encourage, and support others in the pursuit of their dreams and the achievement of their full potential. We call this *coaching with compassion*. We contrast this with *coaching for compliance*, in which a coach attempts to move an individual toward some externally defined objective.

2. Coaching others to truly achieve sustained, desired change requires developing a *resonant relationship* with them. A resonant relationship is one characterized by an authentically compassionate connection and a positive emotional tone.

reflection and application exercise

Reflect on your past and think of the people in your life who have most helped you to grow as a person, motivate and inspire you, and accomplish what you have in life. Think of your whole life, not just work.

Separate the path of your life into distinct stages or eras. These would be approximate time frames that denote major life changes or rites of passage. For many people, this could be as follows:

Life stage 1: Childhood to mid-adolescence (0–14 years)

Life stage 2: High school (15–18 years)

Life stage 3: University, college, military service, or early workforce age (19–24 years)

Life stage 4: Early to mid–working career (25–35 years)

Thereafter, add an additional stage for every block of approximately ten years up to and including your present age. (Please note that the stages listed above should only be used as a rough guide and should be modified according to your own upbringing, cultural background, education, working history, and so forth.)

Create a three-column table with a heading for each column, positioned left to right as: Life Stage, Person's Name or Initials, Notes. In turn, enter into the relevant columns: first, the particular life stage in question; second, the name or initials of the person(s) who inspired you the most at each stage. Third, think of specific events when these people helped you, comments on what they said or did in the event, and how these people made you feel upon reflection (not necessarily at the time). Lastly, what did you learn or take away from these events?

Once you have completed the table, take a few moments to analyze your entries. Are there similarities or differences in how people inspired or motivated you across different life stages or within the same life stages? What is the nature of these differences or similarities? Are there patterns or themes? Write a short paragraph—three hundred words or less—underneath the table articulating the particular patterns you observed and the significance you believe they have had in making you the person you are and the person you aspire to be.

coaching with compassion

inspiring sustained, desired change

People tend to change their behavior *when* they want to change and in the ways they want to change. Without an internal desire to change what or how they behave, any noticeable differences are often short-lived. We've seen this time and again in our observations of managers who coach employees to alter their behavior in order to conform to organizational expectations, or with athletic coaches coaching players to show more commitment to the game by lifting more weights and studying films. We've seen it in how physicians coach their patients around lifestyle changes they should make in the interest of their health and with career coaches who direct their clients to specific opportunities based solely on their skill sets or employment history.

All of those examples describe a common view of coaching—as an activity where, based on your experience, expertise, or authority, you advise individuals on what they should do and how they should do it. While there may be a time and place for it, this type of *coaching for compliance* is unlikely to lead to sustained behavioral change. Just look at the estimated 60–70 percent failure rate of organizational change initiatives, which ultimately rely on individual behavior change.[1] Or look at the nearly 50 percent of chronically ill patients who fail to adhere to their prescribed treatment plans.[2] Being told that we have to or need to change is simply not an effective means of helping us to sustainably alter our behavior.

In this chapter, we will explore in detail the differences between coaching for compliance and coaching with compassion. We will also introduce a five-step process—with coaching with compassion at its core—that's been proved key for creating sustained, desired change. Let's begin with a story that illustrates how one of this book's authors experienced firsthand the power of being coached with compassion versus compliance.

unlocking the power of passion

After nearly fifteen years in sales and marketing management, Melvin decided to return to school full time to pursue a PhD in organizational behavior and human resource management. He was excited at the prospect of teaching at the university level as well as engaging in corporate training and consulting. He quickly learned, however, that the top PhD programs sought to admit students interested in research—not teaching and consulting. In his application, therefore, he took the advice of a professor he knew and presented himself as someone clearly interested in research, but who was also interested in the practical application of that research through teaching and consulting. His strategy was successful, and he was admitted into the doctoral program at the University of Pittsburgh, where he performed well and honed his research skills, positioning himself as a promising scholar.

Upon attaining his doctorate, Melvin landed a tenure-track position at Case Western Reserve University, solidifying his transition into an academic career. During his first year on the faculty, he did what was necessary to establish and pursue his research agenda. By his second year, he'd also been pulled into teaching a couple of programs for executives in addition to his degree-program teaching responsibilities. Before long, he realized that he was spending more and more of his time and attention on teaching, which he enjoyed immensely. He loved inspiring people to apply and use knowledge from his own and his colleagues' research. The enthusiasm his students and program executives felt was electric and contagious. But his research agenda had begun to stall.

During this time, Melvin received informal coaching advice from his department chair and others that he should focus much more on moving his research forward since he'd need to show progress on that front in his upcoming third-year review. He knew this was important and that it was what he ought to be doing, so he began to shift his behavior. He progressed on key research projects and put together a respectable packet for his third-year review, articulating his research agenda and demonstrating his progress. He passed his third-year review but was cautioned about the amount of time he spent on nonresearch activity. Teaching, advising doctoral students, and working with executive education should all be secondary if he hoped to gain tenure.

While he appreciated that advice, Melvin nevertheless found himself continually pulled toward teaching in the degree programs and executive education. Not only did he enjoy helping people learn, but he'd also discovered he was really good at it. He found himself straddling the fence between what he knew he ought to be doing and what his heart told him he really enjoyed. Yet he saw no way around it.

In his fourth year, Melvin had a chance to work formally with a coach as part of a grant-funded program in his department.[3] He anticipated that, as he'd experienced with past coaching, his new coach would focus on what he needed to do to achieve promotion and tenure. But he soon realized that she wasn't pursuing any externally defined agenda whatsoever. She was simply there to help him articulate what he wanted to do and who he wanted to be in the future—as *he* envisioned it—and to help him figure out how to move in that direction.

It didn't take the coach long to identify the tension Melvin had been struggling with for quite some time. On one hand, he expressed a desire to focus on his research for the next few years and earn tenure. On the other hand, however, he wanted to continue, if not expand, the work he'd been doing in executive education. He also expressed a desire to take advantage of the variety of paid speaking opportunities he was now receiving on a fairly regular basis. He hoped it would be possible to "have it all." But he soon understood that to have both, he'd have to postpone teaching and paid speaking opportunities until after tenure, which was still more than five years away, given the school's nine-year tenure process. While he told himself that both the research and teaching were important, he continued to feel frustrated that he wasn't fully applying himself to either endeavor.

While it would have been easy to coach Melvin in the direction that his department and the school encouraged, instead his coach challenged him to identify which way his *heart* was telling him to go. She asked him to engage in a hypothetical exercise.

"What if you had to make a forced choice," she asked, "and in choosing one option, you'd have to forgo the other completely? Under that scenario, which would you choose?" Watching him struggle with the decision, she said, "What if you just choose one and hypothetically try it on—like you would a coat—for a while to see how it feels? If you don't like it, take it off and try on the other one for a while. Then we'll get back together and talk about it."

Melvin "tried on" the research and tenure path first. He imagined what it would be like if he did no executive education or outside speaking engagements at all. He began to pour all of his mental and physical energy into his research. He stayed in that space for a short while, but he soon realized he didn't like how it felt. The thought of remaining in that space for a long period of time was actually uncomfortable. He felt he'd be missing out on something he really wanted to be a part of.

At that point, as his coach had suggested, Melvin switched his mindset toward the executive education and speaking engagement option. Almost immediately, he felt a difference. While the thought of not doing as much research wasn't something he viewed as ideal, he was surprised at how much better this option felt than the previous one. He felt a real excitement about the various activities and opportunities he'd be pursuing with this option.

There was no question what his heart was telling him. "This is it!" he thought.

When he next saw his coach, Melvin shared his new insight, and the remainder of his coaching sessions focused on the steps he'd make to move toward his true passion and ideal vision for his future. Soon he grew comfortable with the fact that he was choosing to primarily teach and speak as opportunities presented themselves. If doing so meant he'd have less time for research—and therefore would be less likely to get tenure—he realized that he could live with that. The research felt like more of a push, something he felt he *ought* to be pursuing, rather than something he wanted deep down inside. His coach had helped him see that.

For the next several months, Melvin was happier than he'd been in quite some time. The tension he'd wrestled with for so long had been lifted. He was pursuing what he wanted to do in his heart and was comfortable with wherever that was leading him. Then, unexpectedly, he was approached about a new position being created at the school—Faculty Director of Executive Education. If he accepted the job, he'd get to play a significant role in growing the school's executive education business. The only catch was that it was a non–tenure track position; to take the job, he'd have to leave the tenure track.

Had it not been for the coaching he'd received and making the discoveries he did about his ideal future, Melvin likely wouldn't have even considered the position. As it turned out, however, he ultimately accepted the job, which he has now enjoyed for more than twelve years. He'll tell anyone who will listen that it was one of the best career decisions he ever made, and that he couldn't have written a better job description for himself. Not only has it allowed him to accept speaking and training engagements throughout the world, but he has also continued to teach in the school's degree programs he enjoys the most while remaining involved with the research and writing projects that truly interest him.

Had Melvin's coach focused on pushing him toward "compliance" rather than compassionately helping him to identify and pursue his vision for his future, imagine how different the outcome might have been. Fortunately, Melvin's coach essentially guided him through five phases, or *discoveries*, of what we call intentional change.

a model for intentional change

A proven method of coaching with compassion in a way that leads to sustained desired change is to guide an individual through Boyatzis's model of intentional change (see figure 3-1). Intentional Change Theory (ICT) is based on the understanding that signifi-

FIGURE 3-1

Boyatzis's Intentional Change Theory in fractals or multiple levels

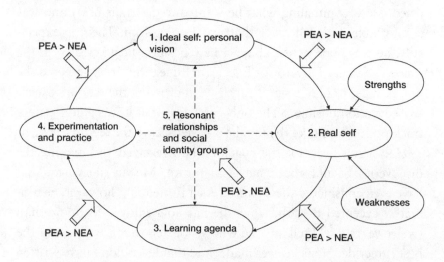

Source: Adapted from R. E. Boyatzis, "Leadership Development from a Complexity Perspective," *Consulting Psychology Journal: Practice and Research* 60, no. 4 (2008), 298–313; R. E. Boyatzis and K. V. Cavanagh, "Leading Change: Developing Emotional, Social, and Cognitive Competencies in Managers during an MBA Program," in *Emotional Intelligence in Education: Integrating Research into Practice,* ed. K. V. Keefer, J. D. A. Parker, and D. H. Saklofske (New York: Springer, 2018), 403–426; R. E. Boyatzis, "Coaching through Intentional Change Theory," in *Professional Coaching: Principles and Practice,* ed. Susan English, Janice Sabatine, and Phillip Brownell (New York: Springer, 2018), 221–230.

cant behavioral change does not take place in a linear fashion. It does not begin with a starting point and then progress smoothly until the desired change has been completed. Instead, behavioral change tends to occur in discontinuous bursts or spurts, which Boyatzis describes as *discoveries*. Five such discoveries must occur for an individual to make a sustained desired change in behavior.[4]

discovery 1: the ideal self

Helping people with the first of these discoveries begins with an exploration and articulation of their *ideal self*, answering such questions as "Who do I really want to be?" and "What do I really want to do with my life?"[5] Note that this is not just about career planning. It is much more holistic. It is about helping people envision an ideal future in all aspects of their life, taking into consideration but not being limited by their current life and career stage. The helper or coach encourages them to draw on their own sense of self-efficacy and tap into feelings of hope and optimism about what might be possible. They will also be encouraged to reflect on their core values, core identity, and what they see as their calling or purpose in life. As a result, they ultimately will be able to articulate a personal vision for their future—and/or a *shared vision* they might have that includes their family, work group, or a larger social cause (more on this below and in chapter 6). (See figure 3-2 for a model of the ideal self.)

When coaching individuals toward discovering their ideal self, be sure they are tapping into who they *really* want to be and what they *really* want to do. Too often, people think they are articulating an ideal self when, in fact, they are describing what could be called an *"ought" self*—who they think they ought to be, or what others think they ought to be doing with their lives. We saw this in Melvin's story: when he was chasing what he thought he ought to do (more research in pursuit of tenure) rather than what he ideally wished for (more teaching and speaking engagements), the energy and enthusiasm needed for a sustained behavior change was just not there.

FIGURE 3-2

Components of the ideal self

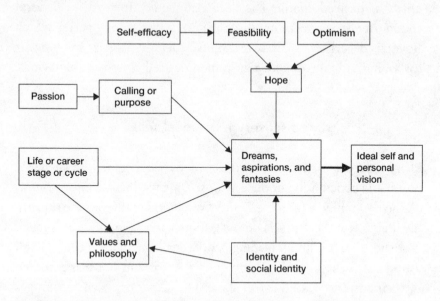

Source: Adapted from R. E. Boyatzis and K. Akrivou, "The Ideal Self as the Driver of Intentional Change," *Journal of Management Development* 25, no. 7 (2006): 624–642.

Helping people genuinely discover their ideal self involves more than guiding them through a series of cognitive or mental exercises. Instead, it is about facilitating a process (often through exercises or reflections, which we will describe here and throughout this book) that leads to an emotional experience where they feel as if a flame has been ignited inside of them around their passion. That's how you and they will know that they have truly tapped into who they are at their best and what they care most deeply about.

An effective way to help people fully explore their ideal self is to have them craft a personal vision statement. We know that when organizations create clear and compelling vision statements that are shared by members of the organization, the results can be positive and powerful. They can help motivate, engage, inspire, and provide a sense of purpose and direction. We believe that a personal vision statement for one's life can be just as meaningful for an individual. The adage, "The odds of hitting your target go up dramatically when you aim at it" sounds obvious. But it's also true: Isn't going through life without a personal vision statement just like shooting at a target without aiming at it?

In some of our programs and courses we show the video *Celebrate What's Right with the World*, narrated by photojournalist and corporate trainer DeWitt Jones.[6] In it, Jones stresses the importance of having a personal vision. He encourages viewers to boil that vision down to a six-word statement that they can memorize and that will inspire them each day. As a coach, that's one of the most powerful things you can do to help people make meaningful, sustained change: help them find the passion and enthusiasm associated with identifying their ideal self and articulating a personal vision statement.

discovery 2: the real self

Coaching people on the second discovery of the intentional change process involves helping them uncover an accurate view of their *real self*. This is not just about assessing strengths and weaknesses. Instead, it is about helping them identify holistically and authentically who they are relative to who they want to be as expressed in their personal vision.

An important role for the coach during this discovery is to help individuals identify the areas of their lives where their ideal self and real self are already aligned. Those areas are their strengths, which can be leveraged later in the change process. Next, the coach should help individuals identify any areas where their real self is *not* currently aligned with their ideal self. These represent gaps that can ideally be closed through targeted behavioral change efforts.

A coach should also help individuals recognize that their real self comprises more than just how they see themselves—they also need to consider how others see them. Some might argue that how others see them is rooted in perception and doesn't necessarily reflect who they really are. But the truth of the matter is that others' collective perceptions of us essentially represent how we show up in the world, which is a key aspect of who we are. Thus, to help the people they are coaching enhance their self-awareness and develop a more comprehensive view of their real self, the coach should suggest they periodically seek feedback from others. In other words, regardless of their intentions, how do others actually perceive them?

When we hear about self-awareness, especially relative to leadership, the focus is often on people's internal self-awareness—their own views of their strengths and weaknesses, as well as their values and aspirations. While important, this focus neglects the other critical aspect of self-awareness: how they are seen by others. Without accurately reading how they are perceived by others, their view of their real self is incomplete.

One way to enhance self-awareness is to receive multi-rater feedback (also known as 360-degree feedback). This process enables individuals to assess themselves on a variety of behaviors, while also being assessed by others from a number of relationships and/or contexts. The traditional view is that comparing one's self-assessment to the assessment of others is a way to gauge one's degree of self-awareness. Our friend and colleague Scott Taylor of Babson College, who has done considerable work in the area of leader self-awareness, suggests that a better indicator of self-awareness is actually people's *prediction* of how others see them measured against how others *actually* see them.[7] A good coach will therefore help individuals being coached gain a greater degree of self-awareness, and hence a better sense of their real self, by helping them develop their capacity to "tune in" and effectively read how they are perceived by others. That way, they can regularly assess how much their *intentions* reflect the actual *impact* they have on others.

Not everyone has the resources or opportunity to participate in a multi-rater feedback assessment process. But there are other ways to accomplish the same goal. First, a coach or other helper can ask individuals to honestly assess the things that they tend to do well (or be good at) and the things they tend to not do so well (or not be so good at). Research suggests that this self-assessment may be biased—but it's still an important part of the process. Next, following the advice of Scott Taylor, the coach should have the individuals predict how others would assess them on key behaviors of interest. And finally, they can actually seek informal feedback from others to see to what extent their predictions of how they're perceived by others match others' actual perceptions.

Having individuals create a "personal balance sheet" (PBS) is another way to help them capture a snapshot of their real self at any point in time, whether or not they have participated in a formal feedback process. With it, they can categorize their short-term and long-term strengths and weaknesses (or development opportunities). They can then weigh those against their ideal self and personal vision statement to determine where they align and where there are gaps. Once they recognize and acknowledge the strengths and gaps between their ideal self and real self, they are ready to move forward with the change process.[8]

The feedback that Melvin received early on as a faculty member suggested he had good teaching and facilitation skills and was an engaging speaker. He recognized those as strengths he could further develop and leverage to become an effective educator and requested speaker. Melvin also received feedback that his research productivity was on the low side. At the time, he had a relatively limited number of active research projects, which were advancing at a moderate pace at best. Had he viewed this feedback in an absolute sense and taken a traditional development path as a result, he would have likely focused his greatest attention on closing the gap represented by a key identified development opportunity—in this case, his research productivity. After working with his coach to clarify his personal vision, however, it became clear that he should direct his energy to working with his identified strengths, which directly supported the most important professional aspects of his vision. That didn't mean ignoring the feedback about his research productivity. He just put it in perspective, deciding to first tap into the positive emotional energy he felt around using his strengths in pursuit of his vision.

This is an important consideration when using a PBS. Often, individuals will immediately turn their attention to the weaknesses and begin thinking of ways to address them. But a compassionate coach can help them see how to make their change efforts more successful—by *first* acknowledging and leveraging their strengths. Only then should they attempt to address any identified weaknesses, focusing primarily on those that help them make the most progress toward their personal vision.

discovery 3: the learning agenda

The third step in the intentional change process is crafting a *learning agenda*. The coach or other helper first asks individuals to revisit the strengths identified in the previous discovery and then think about possible ways those strengths might be utilized to close any relevant gaps. The key here is for people to think about what they're most excited to try in the way of behavior changes to help them grow closer to their ideal self. This is different than a performance improvement plan where they focus on addressing all their shortcomings. That begins to feel like work and can actually inhibit the change process.

Rather, the coach should help individuals recognize that if they continue to do what they've always done, they'll continue to be who they've always been. To change, they'll have to do some things differently. This was the uncomfortable tension Melvin was experiencing— straddling the fence between making teaching or research his first priority. Although he felt that tension, he continued to engage in the same behaviors of not fully committing himself to either path. It was as if he expected that tension to magically disappear over time.

Getting a feel for which path is most exciting is another way to check that you are on the way toward your purpose and vision rather than someone else's notion of what you should do. For example, whenever Melvin was offered the opportunity to design a new learning experience such as a workshop or course, he jumped at it. If it was a choice between designing a new learning experience or working on a research paper, he always chose the learning experience first. This had the most magnetic pull for him. It was a positive attractor that had a stronger pull than the research.

Doing something differently is also the essence of the first half of the fourth discovery (which we'll describe momentarily). It involves experimenting with and then practicing new behaviors. While articulated as a distinct discovery, these experimentation and practice efforts are actually planned for during the creation of the learning agenda. In essence, the third discovery entails planning what one is going to do, whereas the fourth discovery involves putting the plan into action.

discovery 4: experimenting with and practicing new behaviors

This is the fourth discovery in the intentional change process, where the coach encourages the individual to continually try new behaviors and actions, even if they don't always lead to the intended outcome. Experimentation efforts sometimes fail, and that's okay. That's the nature of experimentation. If something doesn't work as anticipated, the coach should encourage the person to either try it again or try something else.

Melvin's coach asked him to focus on one of his two competing professional pathways (teaching/speaking versus research). She challenged him to choose just one, with the understanding that he was doing so at the complete expense of the other. As discussed earlier, Melvin completed the experiment and realized that although he didn't like eliminating research and writing completely, he got an empty feeling when he considered making that the focus of his work. He realized that he *didn't* get that same empty feeling when he placed an exclusive focus on teaching and speaking. He actually felt energized—and this proved to be a breakthrough toward Melvin's sustained desired change.

To trigger the desired "a-ha" of this fourth discovery, the key is to continue experimenting until people find something that works for them. Then the coach can help them shift their experimentation efforts into actual practice, which is the second half of the fourth discovery. At this point, it's critically important to practice and then practice some more. But many people stop short of that, practicing only to the point where they feel comfortable with the new behavior. That's fine for temporary behavior change, but it doesn't work consistently when we are rushed, overwhelmed, angry, sleep-deprived, or under stress and aren't thinking clearly. That's when we're likely to fall back on old behaviors. But if we can keep practicing until we move beyond comfort to the point of mastery, we can change our behavior in truly sustainable ways.

For Melvin, this meant practicing saying "no" to requests to get involved with time-consuming, long-term research projects outside of his primary research area. Previously, he almost always said "yes" to these opportunities because he felt they would help build his research pipeline. Once he developed clarity around his newly articulated focus, however, he had to develop a new habit—being more disciplined with his time and how he responded to such requests, accepting only what interested him the most.

Several researchers and authors have offered views on how long one must practice new behaviors to reach the point of mastery. In his 1960 book *Psycho-Cybernetics*, Maxwell Maltz suggested that it takes at least twenty-one days to form a new habit.[9] Stephen Covey and many others subsequently latched on to that same notion, that habits could be formed in twenty-one days of repeated practice.[10] Malcolm Gladwell, in his 2008 best-seller *Outliers*, suggested that mastery requires about ten thousand hours of practice.[11] Phillippa Lally and her colleagues at University College London studied the topic and found that there was actually considerable variation in how long it took individuals to form a habit, with their study results showing a range of 18 to 254 days.[12]

Regardless of the specific amount of time that's necessary, coaches and other helpers should encourage individuals to practice behaviors they hope to solidify. Individuals being coached should practice the behavior until they don't have to think about it to do it well, when it becomes their new default.

discovery 5: resonant relationships and social identity groups

In coaching to the fifth and final discovery of the intentional change process, a helper or coach helps people recognize that they'll need continued assistance from a network of trusting, supportive relationships with others. Making significant behavioral change can be difficult, and it's even harder in isolation. Change efforts will be more successful when embedded within what we describe as *resonant relationships*, based on genuine, authentic connection that has an overall positive emotional tone. While the connection with the coach or primary helper should be one of those relationships, individuals should also have others they can turn to for support, encouragement, and sometimes accountability. That's what they'll need as they work through each of the discoveries of the intentional change process. We often refer to such a network as a "personal board of directors." Through trusting, supportive relationships along with the formation of social identity groups (more on this in chapter 8), a person benefits from a group of people around her who care and help. These relationships keep the change process alive.

Note that this network of trusting, supportive relationships won't always include the people closest to a person in her everyday life. In fact, sometimes those who are closest to us may not be supportive of a particular change we want to make. That doesn't mean they become less important in our lives. But perhaps they're not who you'll turn to for help on that particular change effort. As our good friend and colleague Daniel Goleman has said in his books and papers, some written with Richard, although emotional and social intelligence is needed at every stage in coaching, establishing and maintaining resonant relationships is perhaps the most crucial.[13]

Such was the case for Melvin when he decided to make a significant career and life change, leaving the corporate world to pursue a PhD and ultimately a career in academia. His wife was his closest and most important relationship, but she was not nearly as excited as he was about the possibility of the change he was contemplating, nor did she have the personal experience and insight into the steps he would need to take to make it happen. He therefore needed to also identify others in his network who might provide relevant coaching and support. Melvin reached out to an old college classmate who'd recently left a career in marketing to pursue her PhD. He also turned to others who had made a similar career shift—including other individuals who were married with children—with whom he could share some of the specific issues of balancing family obligations while transitioning from a corporate job to academia. While Melvin's wife remained the focal relationship in his life, providing support in other areas, his expanded network of trusted supportive relationships helped facilitate his career change effort. Each relationship offered a different perspective and played a unique role in helping him with his desired change.

Such networks of trusted supportive relationships can also help us move forward if we become sidetracked or lose energy or focus around our desired change efforts. For example, a senior executive at a major US financial institution for whom we provided leadership training and executive coaching told us he viewed his identified network as "accountability partners." He asked the people in his network not just to encourage him, but also to support his change efforts by holding him accountable to working on the changes he desired to make.

The coach and these other resonant relationships serve many purposes. In addition to support, one function is what we call *reality testing.* This means helping people get beyond their own blind spots. David Dunning of Cornell University, who studies the process of self-deception, has repeatedly documented how people tend to not know what they don't know.[14] Specifically, without conducting reality testing of other perspectives, people often create delusional misinformation about their own—and others'—expertise and capabilities.

how coaching with compassion works

For nearly three decades, we've been training coaches with an approach based on the Intentional Change Theory, which embodies coaching with compassion. Again and again, we've seen individuals make profound and sustained changes in their lives after being coached in this way. But why and how does it work? And what makes individuals more likely to make and sustain changes in their lives when they are coached in this way?

A number of answers come to mind. For instance, when we use a compassionate approach to help people move toward a self-defined ideal image of their future, our research shows they'll likely change in a sustainable way—far more than when they are told or feel that they have to change. (Of course, it's also possible that people will make a sustained change when it's required, as long as they also feel a genuine, internally driven desire to make that change.) The key here is that the *desire to* motivation for change has to outweigh the *obligation or* motivation.

Recall Emily Sinclair, the soccer player we described in chapter 2. She felt that she ought to put her full attention and effort into developing her skills as a soccer player. It became obvious to her coach that there was something missing from that effort, however. When she shifted her focus to running, which in her heart was what she really wanted to do, her sustained effort to develop as a runner and the result she enjoyed were at an undeniably higher level. Melvin felt that he ought to spend more time focusing on his research agenda. Yet his department chair and others in the school saw clearly that he continually spent time on activities that took him away from his research. When he formally shifted his focus to his teaching and speaking opportunities—what he discovered his heart was telling him he really wanted to do—he flourished in that space. The fact is, individuals most often change sustainably in ways that they want to change, and not in ways that they or others believe that they ought to change.

But there's something else at work here. It turns out that a set of emotional, hormonal, and neurological processes underlie what happens when a person makes sustained change that's driven by a true inner desire. And these are different processes from changes attempted when someone is merely responding to an outside expectation. We will discuss this in greater detail in subsequent chapters. For now, note that coaches and helpers of all kinds play a big role (knowingly or unknowingly) in triggering those emotional, hormonal, and neurological states, and these have a significant impact on an individual's ability to change or even perform.

When coaching for compliance, even if it is well intentioned, a coach often elicits a defensive response from the person being coached. People tend to experience this as a stress response accompanied by negative emotions and activation of the sympathetic nervous system, which in turn triggers a number of hormonal processes that essentially *shut down* the capacity to learn or change in any way. At this point, people have been thrust into the zone of the negative emotional attractor (NEA), which we will cover more in chapter 4. For now we'll say that in this state, people are in survival mode. Their creativity and openness to new ideas are greatly diminished, and the likelihood they'll make or sustain behavioral change is extremely low.

Think about a child in Little League Baseball playing third base in the late innings of a close playoff game. When he makes a throwing error to first base, his coach yells and screams, telling him how stupid and costly a mistake that was and questioning how he could mess up such a simple throw. Suddenly, the horror the player already feels from having made the error is magnified by ten. His stress level goes through the roof. He's now terrified, with a racing heart and shallow, rapid breathing. All he can think about is the gravity of his error, and he prays that the next ball doesn't come to him. But of course, it does. He's now so paralyzed with fear from the corrective "coaching" he's just received that he bobbles a routine ground ball, making yet another error.

This is what often happens with coaching for compliance. Although we may think that we are helping individuals improve their performance, instead we trigger or sustain a stress response. This invokes the NEA, activates the sympathetic nervous system, and actually makes them physically less capable of learning, developing, or favorably changing behavior.

Coaching with compassion elicits a very different response. With a vision of a desired future state and focus on strengths rather than weaknesses, positive emotions are stimulated rather than negative.

The energy and excitement around this positive emotional attractor (PEA) activate the parasympathetic nervous system, which sets into motion a set of physiological responses that put the person in a more relaxed and open state. Creative juices flow. New neural pathways form in the brain, thus paving the way for new learning and sustained behavioral change to occur.

Let's return to our Little League Baseball player, but with a different coach. Upon seeing the boy make a throwing error in the big game, the coach calls a quick timeout. He visits the player at third base, telling him that it is okay. He reminds him to take a deep breath, relax, and get ready for the next batter. He reinforces the fact that he is one of the best third basemen in the league and tells him that he's made that throw a hundred times. All he has to do is think about his mechanics and see himself making a good throw, just as he does 99 percent of the time. After that coaching and reassurance, the player is now calmer, more relaxed and ready for the next play.

This time when the ball comes his way, it's actually not a routine ground ball but rather a tricky play. He won't have time to glove the ball and still make the throw to first. He has to get creative. Thinking quickly, he grabs the ball with his bare hands, sets his feet, squares his shoulders, and makes a beautiful, on-target throw to first base for the out. Because his coach helped him reflect on his strengths and envision a positive outcome, evoking the PEA and activating his parasympathetic nervous system, he was able to relax and think more clearly and creatively.

Although a variety of studies have explored what style of coaching helps individuals the most, the difference we are discussing is deeper than behavioral style.[15] For example, our colleague Carol Kauffman advocates using flexibility in integrating various approaches from behavioral and psychoanalytic therapy to coaching.[16] A major difference is that we are examining what the *individual experiences*, not just the coach's intention.

As we've said, we have collected considerable empirical evidence supporting the effectiveness of coaching with compassion in bringing about sustained desired change in individuals.[17] We have also gathered over time a great deal of anecdotal evidence on the power of this approach in helping individuals make meaningful changes in their lives.

For several years, we collected responses from managers, executives, and advanced professionals on the reflection and application exercise in chapter 2. When these individuals shared reflections about the people who had helped them most in their lives, they were consistently filled with warm, emotional reactions to those memories. Whether tender or challenging, those moments had a lasting impact largely because of the genuine care and concern the individuals showed them. When we coded these shared reflections for which aspects of the intentional change process were primarily involved, we found that approximately 80 percent of the moments people recalled involved someone helping them tap into their dreams, aspirations, core values, and/or strengths. In essence, they helped them discover their ideal self or appreciate their distinctive capabilities.

Conversely, when we asked them to recall people who had *tried* to help them, but who were not necessarily successful in doing so, we found that well over half of the instances recalled involved someone giving them feedback on areas where they needed to improve. In other words, they focused on their gaps or weaknesses.[18] Given these observations, it is no surprise that so many individuals fail to change in sustained ways. Too often, the people trying to help them unknowingly trigger a stress response, tipping them into the negative emotional attractor and making them physically less capable of making change.

To be an effective coach or successfully work in a helping role of any kind, you can't get around the critical role that emotions play in people's change efforts. Coaches need to become experts at recognizing and skillfully managing the emotional flow of the coaching process. This requires being tuned into the person being coached, creating a sense of synchrony that allows you as a coach to read as well as influence the emotions the person is experiencing. Additionally, given the role of emotional contagion, being able to effectively manage the emotional tone of the coaching discussion also requires having an awareness of one's own emotions—and recognizing the impact that they can have on the person being coached. We'll discuss this more in chapter 7.

———————

In this chapter, along with the reflection and application exercises, we introduce conversation guides. Like the exercises, the guides are designed to have you reflect on the topics discussed in the chapter. However, since meaningful conversations are at the heart of helping, we strongly encourage you to find others with whom you can have conversations about these topics; the conversation guides are designed to help start those exchanges. You may also find it helpful to discuss the reflection and application exercises with others. The more you discuss these topics with others, the better!

In chapter 4, we will continue exploring the PEA and NEA and look further at how the brain affects the coaching process.

key learning points

1. Coaching with compassion begins by helping a person explore and clearly articulate her ideal self and a personal vision for her future. This often means helping her tease out the distinction between her "ideal" self and "ought" self.

2. To help individuals build self-awareness, ensure that they consider their strengths and weaknesses in the context of their personal vision statement first. A useful tool for this is the personal balance sheet (PBS). The PBS guides the individual to consider assets (strengths) and liabilities (gaps or weaknesses). To ignite the energy for change, coaches should encourage those they help to focus two to three times more attention on strengths than weaknesses.

3. Rather than creating performance improvement plans in which individuals focus on their shortcomings, the learning agenda should focus on behavior changes that they feel most excited to try—changes that would help them grow closer to their ideal self.

4. Coaches should encourage individuals to practice new behaviors beyond the point of comfort. Only continual practice leads to mastery.

5. Rather than relying solely on a coach for support, individuals need to develop a network of trusted, supportive relationships to assist them in their change efforts.

6. Coaches must be aware of and effectively manage the emotional tone of the coaching conversations.

reflection and application exercises

1. Thinking back over the course of your life, what were the situations and events in which you truly acted "on your own terms" and didn't feel you were purely reacting to others or doing what others wanted you to do? Have there been times where you have felt genuinely self-directed in pursuit of your own dreams and aspirations? Was there a shift in life philosophy, personal values, or general outlook that preceded these times? How did these times in your life feel?

2. Have there been times in the past where you felt a disconnect between the person you would like to be and the person you were? Have you ever seriously compromised your values to please others? Have you ever seriously compromised your own values or ideals for the sake of being practical or expedient? How did you feel in such moments?

3. Think about a coach or someone else who brought out the best in you. How did you feel about what you were doing and why you were doing it?

4. Think about a coach or someone else who tried to get you to do something you really didn't want to do. How did that feel? Did you change in the requested direction? If so, how long did the change last?

conversation guide

1. When in your life have you attempted to coach or help someone change his behavior in a way that you wanted him to change? How was that received? How much did the person change? To what extent was that change in behavior sustained?

2. When have you had conversations aimed at helping people discover and pursue something they were really excited to do? How did those conversations go? To what extent did those people make sustained progress toward their desired change?

3. What type of coaching do you observe most often in your organization—coaching with compassion or coaching for compliance? Why do you think that is the case? What is the collective impact of this on the organization?

awakening the desire to change

questions that spark joy,

gratitude, and curiosity

When Aaron Banay (not his real name) was in his third week of kindergarten, his teacher asked everyone to draw a picture of a house. In figure 4-1, you can see the typical drawing made by other children in the class, and then Aaron's drawing (all drawings have been converted to black and white for reproduction).

Later the teacher asked everyone to draw an airplane. In figure 4-2, we show a drawing of the typical student in the class, and then Aaron's drawing.

After looking at Aaron's drawings, the teacher talked to the school principal. Despite Aaron's engaging smile and easy manner with others, the two educators determined that the drawings—. along with Aaron's slight resistance to the teacher's guidance in the classroom and seeming somewhat withdrawn from others—were

FIGURE 4-1

House

By most kindergartners

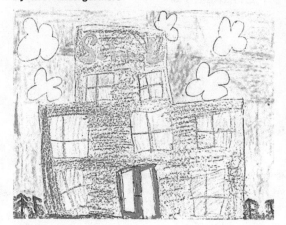

By Aaron

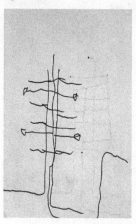

FIGURE 4-2

Airplane

By most kindergartners

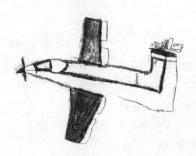

By Aaron

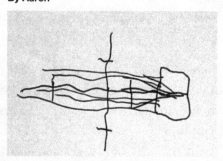

possible evidence of emotional troubles, difficulties at home, or learning disabilities. They believed a clinical psychologist might even see these drawings as a view of the world separated from reality.

After a series of their own conferences, they called Aaron's parents for a special meeting. The teacher and principal showed Joseph and Allison Banay (not their real names) their son's drawings and expressed their concern. They then handed Aaron's parents an affidavit saying that their child should be placed in a special needs program that the county had available. Joseph and Allison were angry and confused. They explained that their home life was going well, and Aaron showed no indication of emotional problems. But the teacher said she was worried he wouldn't be able to keep up in school and that he'd hold the others back.

What she didn't tell them was that she was trying to get Aaron to write with his right hand, and he was resisting. As a result, she'd stopped giving Aaron the same attention she gave to the other children, and Aaron was feeling isolated. Joseph and Allison knew none of this at that moment. But the teacher and principal had aroused every parent's fear that something might be very wrong with their child, and they felt defensive. They knew Aaron was the youngest in his class, but they also knew he was a curious, engaging, and eager child at home. They argued that he should be given a chance. But the teacher and principal insisted he be assigned to a new special class.

Joseph and Allison left the meeting feeling dejected and bullied into a decision that could affect their son's development and future. Were they being defensive and closed to an important possibility? Or were the teacher and principal being closed to a different interpretation?

When his parents returned home, Aaron saw they were holding his two pictures. His face lit up and he asked them what they thought of his drawings. His parents were, of course, still trying to grasp what was going on. That's when Joseph, an internal consultant at a large company, decided to ask Aaron what *he* thought about his drawings.

Both parents sat down with Aaron and told him they loved the pictures. Then with an encouraging smile, Joseph asked his son what he saw and why he drew the pictures the way he did. Aaron eagerly pointed to the lines in the house and airplane and said, "You can't have a building without electrical and plumbing, and you can't have a plane without the hydraulics and the electrical system. If I drew the outside first, you would never see all the important stuff inside."

His mother and father were astonished. By asking him a simple question—"What do you see?"—they discovered that their son was a budding architect or engineer with a complex view of a house and an airplane—far more complex than a typical five-year-old's view. He was not a learning-disabled, emotionally disturbed child. Rather, he showed the analytic brilliance of a gifted child.

After the fact, it is easy to read this moment in the Banays' life and say, "Of course, the educational experts were being narrow-minded." But in an emotionally charged meeting in which they aroused negative emotions in everyone present, the "experts" believed they were correct and that Aaron's parents were being the usual, defensive parents protesting that their child was special, smart, and sensitive. It took Joseph the relatively simple task of asking Aaron the right question to discover a different truth and a dramatically different assessment of the situation and what was needed to help Aaron grow and develop. Sadly, it took another two years to get the educational experts in this school system to change their position and move Aaron back into the regular classroom with his friends. By then the teacher and principal had probably slowed Aaron's growth by diverting him into special-needs classes based on their assumption that he was troubled.

Our point is this: to help other people, we have to focus on *them*, not on our vision of how we think things should be. We have to understand them. To understand them, we have to talk to them and discover their views of the world, their situation, and how they feel. It's true— to effectively coach or help anyone, we need to find out what the other person is *feeling* as well as *thinking*. Sadly, what the other person is thinking is often assumed, especially by people in professional helping roles.

This is a central challenge. As coaches and helpers, we actually *are* often more experienced and perhaps even more knowledgeable. But our mistake is in thinking—and often assuming—that we can see what the person should do to lead a better life, be more pro-ductive, or learn more. That was the trap that the educators in

Aaron's story fell into. In trying to *fix* Aaron's situation and his parents' perception of their son, they triggered a negative response from the Banays, who experienced the encounter as negative evaluation of their son and an imposition of something they *should* do. And of course they weren't even sure they agreed with the action proposed. For them, the whole conversation was what we'd call an *NEA moment*—their negative emotional attractors were triggered, putting them on high alert and hindering their ability to respond (at least in that moment) in a productive way.

In this chapter, we will look at how to ask the right questions to create the tipping points that can lead to sustainable change, and how focusing on the wrong things essentially blocks change. We'll explore how to invoke the positive emotional attractor (PEA) for maximum growth—and how the positive can become blocked in individuals, sometimes by the very people who are trying to help them. We also offer specific ways to tap into positive emotions that will keep both the helper and the person being helped in a state that's receptive to growth and sustainable change. Finally, you'll find at the end of the chapter an exercise for tracking your emotions over time and looking for patterns related to PEA and NEA.

awakening the PEA

A coach who asks thought-provoking questions ("What do you see in your drawing?" "What's important to you in your life?") can awaken a person's PEA, activating parts of the brain that trigger hormones— the *parasympathetic nervous system* (PNS)—that is associated with emotions such as awe, joy, gratitude, and curiosity. Asking the wrong questions (focusing on things like what an airplane "should" look like in a drawing, or what's required to get a promotion) arouses a person's NEA, activating different brain networks and triggering hormones that activate the *sympathetic nervous system* (SNS) and thus the fear and anxiety associated with the human fight-or-flight response. In fact, studies show that just anticipating a negative event (e.g., thinking about what you "ought" to do), can arouse the NEA!

It's not surprising, therefore, that asking the right questions ulti-mately opens people up to what's possible in their lives, includ-ing sustainable change. Yet many coaches and other helpers fail to do that. Instead, they coach for compliance in the ways we've described in Aaron's story and elsewhere in this book.

When we coach with compassion, we begin by asking the person to articulate his *ideal self* or vision for himself. This anchors him in the PEA, encouraging openness and creativity and producing an experience of excitement that can come with change. As we learned in chapter 3 and will elaborate in more detail in this chapter, the PEA essentially acts as a tipping point that helps a person move from one step to another along the five discoveries in our model for intentional change, ultimately leading to sustained desired change.

In Aaron's case, neither of the "experts" asked questions to understand Aaron's thoughts when he made his drawings. So his experience was one of being misunderstood—not because he hadn't communicated or had done so improperly, but because the educa-tors didn't think to ask him a simple question about *his* perspective. Similarly, coaches and people helping others often become preoccu-pied with what they think the other person should do and slide into coaching for compliance. Think of the doctor advising a patient to quit smoking, or a manager advising an employee to learn a certain skill that may not be remotely interesting to her. Even with the best intentions, these attempts typically fail because they arouse defen-siveness in the other person and a sense of obligation—that is, the "ought" self.

In educational settings such as Aaron's classroom, this is called focusing on teaching (what the teachers and administrators have to say) rather than learning (what the students are actually learning).[1] In such a setting, education is framed as an expert system, with the teachers and administrators knowing more about the process than the students or parents. Historically, this has not worked well in education, and as we are asserting in this book, it is unhelpful in any coaching situation.[2]

Of course, this does not mean that as coaches we have to cleanse our minds of what we know might be good for the people we are trying to help. But it does mean we need to exercise emotional self-control.[3] In other words, can you as a coach withhold your advice long enough to discover what is on the mind of the person you're trying to help?

Joseph Banay would not have had the chance to hear Aaron's intent in the drawings if he had asked an all-too-common parental query, "What were you thinking?!" Or the other common question, "Why didn't you draw it like the other kids in the class?" These questions are asked all too often with the intent of getting others to defend themselves or their actions. Naturally, such questions immediately put people on the defensive and into the NEA. They induce stress in people on the receiving end.

But asking another type of question, especially an open-ended one, can bring people into the PEA and a more open-minded state. In management research circles, this type of positive or open-ended question is what's known as an *outward mindset*, in contrast to an *inward mindset*. It brings you outside of yourself. With that comes some relief from worrying about your troubles. Besides giving some symptom relief from a preoccupation with yourself, it increases your ability to scan the interpersonal environment around you. Another way of saying this is that even for the people being coached or helped, predominantly focusing on others helps to produce more change than predominantly focusing on themselves. In chapter 5, we will explain the neurological basis for this.

In his magnificent book *Helping*, Ed Schein, an emeritus professor at MIT and leader in the field for more than sixty years, calls questions without an implicit desired answer "humble inquiry."[4] In examining all forms of helping, which he sees as similar to each other, Schein recommends paying attention to the inherent status differences in any formal or informal helping situation and the conscious or unconscious expectation of some exchange. Part of the objective in helping, he says, is to help the other person regain some status, which gives them confidence and provides "as much data as possible for both." One of his principles is that "everything you say or do is an intervention that determines the future of the relationship." The best relationship is one that is both equitable and full of mutual trust. Schein recommends that we would learn more from another person and encourage more of their own self-exploration and ownership of the learning process if we engaged in humble inquiry—asking questions without an imbedded answer. In our language, such inquiry would more likely help someone into the PEA than the alternatives.

One of us recently watched an exchange in a training program at a midsized manufacturing company. During a discussion about a coaching exercise, one high-potential manager said, "We are not used to asking others about their feelings." Whether because it seems too personal or gushy, this company culture ignores the emotional drivers of people's motivation, engagement, and mood. The company leaders ignore the dangers of the emotional contagion we described in chapter 2, in which "leaders and managers infect others with their moods and feelings without understanding or dealing with the consequences."

Recall the story of Kyle Schwartz (chapter 1), the teacher who asked for her students' response to the statement "I wish my teacher knew . . ."[5] This is a great example of asking the right question. From her students' responses (e.g., "I wish my teacher knew that my family and I live in a shelter"), Schwartz learned what they were dealing with outside of the classroom, which helped her understand how to best teach them. For their part, the students understood that their teacher cared about their lives and feelings, putting them in a positive frame of mind to learn.

focusing on the wrong things

Unlike the positive opening to learning that occurs when we ask the right questions, people tend to shut down when, in our interactions, we focus on the wrong things. One of this book's authors (Richard) had this experience:

> I was working on a research paper in my home office when my wife came in. She walked over to the window that faces

the street and asked if I'd seen the large front loader that the gas company had brought to install new pipelines. Without turning from my computer, I said, "What?" in a somewhat annoyed voice. To which my wife responded, in a calm voice, "That wasn't very nice." Completely exasperated now, I said in a raised voice: "I'm writing about emotional intelligence. I don't have time for doing that!" My wife stared at me in disbelief. At that point, I leaned back in my chair and laughed, realizing what she already knew—the absurdity of what I'd just said to her, in all earnestness.

In the interaction with his wife, Richard was clearly focused on the wrong thing. How could he hope to convey emotional intelligence to his readers if he couldn't practice those skills with his own wife? This is a classic problem in attention.[6] We need to focus to get things done or analyze a situation, but in focusing on one thing, we preclude our ability to be aware of or even see things around us. The mere act of looking to the north means that we might not see a bird flying to the south. By focusing on our company's internal production efficiency, we may not see a competitor's new product launch that will threaten one of our main product lines. By focusing on handling more email, we might not see that our daughter is sad and needs a hug.

When such focusing becomes our typical behavior, it turns into a habit, and habits are difficult to break or even interrupt. Although they lack the biochemical addictive nature of smoking a cigarette, drinking coffee, or having a few beers after work, the focus on only some aspects of our situation (like work or an addiction)—to the exclusion of others (like our health, our spouses, or our children)—tends to restrict our field of vision. We essentially become blind to what might actually matter most in a particular situation.

Coaching, like any form of helping, is also a focused pursuit. But what we are advocating is coaching that focuses on *the other person* (in a management context, the "subordinate" and in educational terms, the "learner") rather than on some external agenda (an emphasis on "directing" or "teaching" itself). Accordingly, the best coaches help a person by guiding her focus, helping her notice what she's feeling as well as noticing the people around her and aspects of situations she might otherwise have missed. That kind of focus helps her enter an experience or state of the PEA—the neurological, hormonal, and emotional state in which we are more open to new ideas, other people, moral concerns, and are able to scan our environment to notice patterns or themes. Such openness seems essential if we are to learn or adapt new behaviors and actions.

Yet as we've illustrated in this book, the most common way people try to help or coach someone does exactly the opposite. We see this in organizations we work with every day. Because most organizational cultures tend to overemphasize analytics, the brains of people in those companies continually operate in NEA moments—leading to a state of varying degrees of cognitive, perceptual, and emotional impairment.

Such was the case with Richard in our example. While working on his paper, he hardly noticed when his wife entered his office. His eyes, ears, and every sense were fixed on the words on his computer. At the same time, he was anticipating the criticism of academic reviewers and trying to figure out how to avoid or minimize their wrath. Yet he was also excited about the results he and his research partners were revealing about how emotional intelligence affects engineers' effectiveness.[7] All of this was raging in Richard's mind and increasing his focus on the computer screen and detracting from his ability to notice anything else in the room. In a real sense, Richard at that moment was perceptually impaired—and unable to interact positively with someone he loves dearly. And because he was apparently in an NEA state, he was possibly less creative and couldn't use his typical cognitive ability in editing the research paper.

Another form of the wrong focus is using sympathy rather than empathy—feeling bad for the other person rather than trying to understand them. As we will discuss in chapter 7, there are several forms of empathy. And empathy is only one component of what we mean by acting with compassion. As nineteenth-century explorer David Livingstone is quoted as saying, "Sympathy is not a substitute for action." Excessive sympathy for another person may become a form of enabling their negativity and focus on their problems instead of possibilities.[8]

invoking the PEA

As someone focused on the person you're helping, you will need to ask questions to draw out what he is thinking and feeling. Asking the right question at the right time can make a tremendous difference—as it did in the following conversations.

Darryl Gresham was doing quite well by society's standards. He was in a job he loved as VP of information technology at a middle-sized company. His relationship with his daughter was comfortable and loving, and he was financially supporting her college and graduate school education. Although Darryl had a girlfriend, he had a friendly relationship with his ex-wife. He was active in the national Promise Keepers organization and his local church. Compared with most of his childhood friends, he was living a dream. The tough neighborhood in which he was raised in Cleveland didn't have many VPs of industry as alumni—at least, who'd survived black nationalist and Black Panther organizations.

Having arrived at a stage of life where he felt somewhat restless, Darryl enrolled in a leadership program. One of the components of the program was the opportunity to meet with a coach to discuss his future aspirations and the results from a 360-degree assessment of his emotional intelligence behavior, and convert it all into a detailed learning plan for the coming five to ten years.[9] Each executive began by writing a personal vision essay, which the coach reviewed before meeting to discuss it.

Darryl's coach found his essay challenging. Instead of addressing the comprehensive aspects of his life, as requested (his personal relationships, family, community, spiritual and physical health, as well as work), Darryl focused his entire essay on his family and community. Among the fast-track executives in this program, the lack of any mention of his work and future career was highly unusual. The coach sent Darryl an email and jokingly asked if he had a lucrative trust fund. But privately, the coach suspected there was something holding Darryl back from exploring his desired career future. Perhaps he was feeling stuck or had hit a midlife crisis and had lost the excitement he'd found in his early work years.

When they met, the coach asked Darryl to describe his dreams and his vision about work. Darryl responded with a blank stare. So the coach asked about his near-term vision of a desired future. After a long silence, Darryl shrugged his shoulders. But then the coach remembered a specific exercise used to stimulate reflection about one's dreams and vision. "If you won the lottery, say $80 million dollars," he asked, "how would it affect your work or life?"

Darryl responded easily to that question. He said he would set aside enough for his daughter to complete college and graduate school, and he'd create a fund for his ex-wife.

"And what would you do for work?" asked the coach.

Darryl didn't hesitate: "I'd drive a truck cross-country." Darryl had worked for Roadway Package Systems during his late twenties, thus his love of cross-country truck driving.

From the coach's perspective, Darryl seemed to be describing more of an escape fantasy than a real dream. He was sure he hadn't yet tapped into Darryl's PEA—the important positive state that would tip him into being open to visualize his desired future. But as it later became clear, Darryl did in fact want to escape from work because this aspect of his life had become routine and boring. Moreover, he experienced racism at work that was a constant burden and was hard to communicate even with his coach.

As he worked with Darryl in this coaching session, the coach tried a number of specific exercises. When he asked Darryl to describe his "bucket list" and "a fantasy job," both drew blank stares. He was stuck. This was NEA territory, the coach was certain.

The coach decided to approach the topic from a different angle. "Let's dream a little," the coach said. "You have just had a great week. You go home and pour yourself a drink and sit down. There's a smile on your face. You feel you've been doing important and good work this past week." The coach paused and let Darryl get into the fantasy. He could see his face relax.

The coach asked, "What had you done that was so fulfilling?"

Darryl did not skip a beat: "Teaching high-school kids in the inner city that computers can be their instruments to freedom." Suddenly, Darryl's entire demeanor changed. His eyes brightened, he leaned forward, and he started talking faster than the coach had heard in months. He was in the PEA zone. The clarity of the image in the dream and its comprehensiveness was erupting. The excitement was contagious—the coach could see and feel that Darryl had just had an epiphany. Possibilities opened. He talked about how he might teach workshops in the evening or on weekends at local high schools. He talked about setting up IT internships for high school students at local companies. It was as if a dam had opened and ideas were pouring out. His image of his career and future changed from "Been there, done that," to "Wow, I can't wait to get started!" Darryl now had a dream of what he could be and do. He even had some good ideas about how to get there.

But then, like a fire that had been doused with a hose, his expression turned negative again and he said, "But I can't do that." The coach asked, "Why?" and Darryl answered that he needed the money that he was making to provide for his daughter, ex-wife, and his own current lifestyle. He even apologized for feeling that way.

The coach asked him why he thought it was an all-or-nothing move. Darryl turned his head with a quizzical look. The coach said, "You don't have to give up your day job to do this work. What about doing it on the side, a day a month or even a day a week? Do you think you could do some workshops at the same high school you attended and still fulfill all of your current duties?"

Darryl's hopeful demeanor returned. He smiled and said, "Sure!" He spent another fifteen minutes brainstorming different ways to approach this dream.

A few months later, Darryl called his coach and said he'd been asked to teach some IT courses at a local community college. He jumped at the chance and was able to do it in his spare time. In later communications with his coach, he described several moves, including taking a job closer to his hometown to help his ailing mother. The new job was in mergers and acquisitions, but he did it eagerly. After a few years, he was offered a promotion to global logistics.

Although he hadn't yet begun offering workshops in high schools, Darryl kept the dream alive by actively mentoring young people hired into his company in various functions. He noticed that many of them needed basic living skills, like managing money, so Darryl organized workshops at his company to teach these life and career skills. All of this was in addition to his regular job, but with the company's sanction. The other interesting change Darryl noted was that his interest had spread to helping all of the young, new hires at his workplace, regardless of their racial or socioeconomic background. Today, he looks forward to some formal teaching at community colleges in the area.

Let's review this process: The coach's first challenge was to find a way to bring Darryl into the PEA. As long as he remained stuck in the NEA, Darryl could not see his options. In fact, his brain was actually working against him by being defensive and protecting him from potentially harmful thoughts or dreams. But once the coach found a way to help Darryl invoke his PEA, it was like a dam of cognitive and emotional concrete had burst. Darryl was ready and eager to move ahead with all aspects of this life. Entering the PEA and feeling a feasible, hopeful way to live his dream enabled him to use the rest of his talent to sort out how best to get there.

This is how the coach used a variety of ways to invoke the PEA and finally hit upon the one that worked for Darryl at that moment in his life. Most importantly, the coach had to withhold the desire to "fix" Darryl, and that required patience and humility—and sometimes silence while he waited for Darryl to frame his thoughts and share them. (We offer a more detailed discussion of the best questions to ask to invoke the PEA in chapter 7.) This is how the coach helped to create a tipping point from Darryl's NEA state to an open PEA state. Once Darryl identified his steps, he felt his passion and felt renewed, safe, open, and even curious. He could try these steps to analyze their feasibility. He could go in and out of the NEA, but under his own control because he had a guiding vision. In other words, before he could begin to make a plan, Darryl needed to articulate his dream.

In this way, the PEA is an experience in which you feel open to others and new ideas, but it is also a tipping point. It can invoke a new stage in the change process or a new step in increasing awareness. A tipping point is technically a phase transition, like ice moving from a solid state to a liquid state of flowing water. The temperature at which the ice cube begins to melt is a tipping point.

Unfortunately, that's not always what occurs when one person tries to help another.

when helpers hinder positive change

Often, when a coaching conversation begins, the person being helped arrives in a state of frustration and therefore might spend some time venting or expressing listlessness, as we saw with Darryl Gresham. In those cases, it's important that the coach expresses empathy so that the other person knows he is being supported. But many training programs teach people in helping roles to go too far, shifting from validating the person's feelings to becoming an *enabler* of the NEA. Allowing someone to wallow in her NEA is not helping or supporting her. Rather, she will begin to feel more stressed, not less, and become cognitively impaired, less open to new ideas for change and learning.

Take for example a growing public policy problem—obesity and the related insulin resistance and Type II diabetes. If you've ever been volume-challenged, we are sure you've tried a diet. You might have tried several. For most people, weight loss from the diet brings joy, but then in the coming months or years, they regain the weight. Why? Because the benefits of most diets are short-lived. If you try to lose weight, studies show that you'll likely fail to sustain any weight you lose. The difficulty is that "losing weight" is a negatively framed goal. Trying to limit or change what and how much you eat requires a lot of self-control, which activates the NEA and is stressful.[10] No matter how much you repeat, "I need to do this," it is hard to sustain the effort needed to stick to the plan.

Doctors and nurses often don't help much in the quest to change behavior. They easily fall victim to their intent and the leap to trying to tell someone what they should do. This invites more NEA than PEA, and the helper becomes an enabler of the poor or inappropriate—certainly less desired—behavior. If you've ever been told by a doctor that you have a condition requiring a behavior change, you've likely left the doctor's office concerned, maybe frustrated and worried. Type II diabetes has a treatment adherence of about 50 percent in the United States and around the world.[11] That means that people do about half of the things the doctor or nurse tells them to do. How could people be so foolish?

The NEA is the culprit. Once in the NEA, you are exerting effort in a mental state of closing down. Your body wants to defend itself, and you want to say, "Enough! I need that doughnut!" At that moment, you actually do not need the doughnut. Rather, to start a change or learning process, you need to enter the PEA. This is difficult to do by yourself. That's why the most effective coaches learn ways to help people enter the PEA, feel hope, and begin a process of change. Two prominent doctors, Jerome Groopman and Atul Gawande, have written about the role of hope in medical settings. Even in situations of palliative care, there can be hope—not necessarily for miraculous healing, but rather hope around the quality of the patient's life in the time remaining.[12]

how to invite the positive attractor

As we saw in the example of Darryl Gresham, coaches and others such as managers, parents, and teachers can use a number of methods to help another person experience a sense of hope and thereby initiate a PEA tipping point. These include asking about a person's dreams and vision; using compassion; using emotional contagion; practicing mindfulness; invoking playfulness; walking in nature; and developing a resonant coaching relationship.

dreams and personal vision

The first way to invite the PEA is to help a person feel hopeful about the future. You can do this by asking a person about his dreams and personal vision. An fMRI study showed that spending thirty minutes in a conversation about a person's vision or dream activates regions of the brain associated with imagining new things and more PNS activity (the parasympathetic nervous system, described earlier in this chapter, which is associated with emotions such as awe, joy, gratitude, and curiosity).[13]

use of compassion

Another powerful experience that simulates the PEA is receiving or expressing compassion or caring for another. We can experience this by helping others less fortunate or in need. We also can feel compassion by feeling grateful to others for how they have helped us. As we discussed in chapter 2, reflecting on the people who have helped you in your life invokes gratitude and the PEA. Talking about these relationships with others makes the experience of the PEA more intense. Being in a loving relationship is another powerful way to maintain compassion in your daily life. Stimulation of compassion allows us to care about others. The act of caring takes us away from our own world view to another person's experience. This goes beyond empathy to wanting to do something for the other person. People often report that when they feel cared for by another, they return the feeling and extend care back to the other person.

One of the earliest documented ways to invoke compassion is having a pet, like a dog, cat, horse, or monkey (it does not seem to

research spotlight

Research shows that stress activates the sympathetic nervous system (SNS).[14] This is true whether the stress is annoying but mild, or whether it's acute. When stressed, your body secretes epinephrine and norepinephrine (adrenaline/noradrenaline) at dosage levels that act as vasoconstrictors. This sends blood from distal capillaries and extremities to large muscles groups needed for survival (epinephrine to your arms; norepinephrine to your legs). As a result, your pulse rate and blood pressure increase, and your breathing gets faster and shallower. You also secrete corticosteroids, and eventually cortisol enters your blood stream. Besides being a natural anti-inflammatory, cortisol diminishes the functioning of your immune system and inhibits neurogenesis. Chronic, annoying stress (such as working under a demanding or toxic boss) causes your body to activate and prepare to defend itself but also results in cognitive, perceptual, and emotional impairment.

In contrast, research shows that the parasympathetic nervous system (PNS) activates renewal processes, including stimulation of the vagus nerve and secretion of oxytocin (primarily in females) and vasopressin (primarily in males). At this dosage level, these are vasodilators. They open your blood flow; as a result, you feel warmer, your blood pressure and pulse rate drop, your breathing slows down and gets deeper. You engage your immune system to its fullest capability. Without such regular and periodic renewal experiences, chronic stress will make your functioning and performance nonsustainable.

work the same way with fish or birds). By stroking or petting them, you can invoke your PEA.[15] This actually begins by stimulating PEA in the pet, and because of emotional contagion at the unconscious level, it quickly spreads to you, the person doing petting, and then back to the pet, and so on, in a positive feedback loop.

An earlier book by Richard Boyatzis and Annie McKee, *Resonant Leadership*, recounted the story of Mark Scott, a young executive in a mortgage bank who wanted to help the famous football team of his alma mater—the University of Georgia.[16] He approached Coach Richt with the idea of having them build a Habitat for Humanity house for a needy family. It worked amazingly well. The team soon decided to build one or two each year, and the idea spread to other athletic teams at UGA and even to other schools in the area. The benefit was not merely a public relations move, nor was it just "team building" off the field; rather, it gave the players a chance to do something good for others. This experience of the PEA through compassion helped the college players step outside of themselves and focus other people—not team members, not opponents, but rather a family from their town whom they did not know before the day of the Habitat project.

emotional contagion

Our brains are hardwired for picking up on the emotions of others around us. But sensing negative emotions may stimulate the SNS and turn the person defensive. Except for people with autism spectrum disorder, this is true of all humans. A person may have developed techniques to tune out the message, as Richard did with his wife's statement about the front loader in their yard. But the circuitry is still there.

The surprising aspect about sensing others' deep feelings is not that we all have some form of what used to be called telepathic ability. It is how fast it happens. The psychologist Joseph LeDoux documented that it takes about 8 milliseconds for the message of a threat to go from our five senses to the amygdala.[17] That is eight-thousandths of a second. This is way below consciousness or conscious recognition, which is typically thought to be about 500 milliseconds, or half a second.[18] That's one reason it's so important for coaches to be aware of their own emotions and tend to them, before entering any situation in which they hope to help others. Emotional contagion is a real phenomenon!

Mark Scott was using positive emotional contagion to help the team build a sense of purpose and caring. Coaches and other helpers do it all the time. But the coach's own feelings might transmit a different feeling than their intent. If the coach is still upset about an argument with his or her partner, the negative emotions may infect the person being coached, regardless of what they were discussing.

mindfulness

Another approach to the PEA is through mindfulness: being tuned into and aware of yourself, others around you, and the natural environment. It is focusing on your context. Decades ago, advice to the stressed was to take time and "smell the roses." Today, overworked people might practice meditation, prayer, or yoga, or do regular physical exercise that is repetitive, like running. The key is to invoke the PEA by using these techniques to *center oneself*. (An interesting side note, prayer works well but it seems to be important that a person is praying to a loving God, not a vengeful one.[19]) Keeping a fish tank might invoke the PEA—that is, watching fish for periods of time may allow you to create a meditative state.

playfulness

A few years ago, we saw an increased body of research showing that playfulness, joy, and laughter invokes the PNS and, by extension, the PEA. Our friend Fabio Sala showed in his PhD thesis that the form of humor most likely to have this positive effect is self-deprecating humor—not the kind that makes fun of others.[20]

For example, think about a time when you were at an event with friends or family and enjoyed laughing together. How did you feel when you left the event?

We suspect that playfulness works because it reminds us of our humility and vulnerabilities but lowers the intensity of the threat. By making fun of it, by laughing, we make it seem less serious. The stimulation of the PEA may allow us to see the context, or the bigger picture and not focus on the negative moment.

walking in nature

The most recently added activity that appears to stimulate the PNS (and therefore the PEA) is walking in nature, perhaps because it stimulates mindfulness.[21] The act of walking in the woods (assuming we are not texting or checking email) expands our perception and senses about the world around us—nature, animals, the weather. It is an expanding circle of awareness.

a resonant helping/coaching relationship

Beyond the desirability of helping another person get into the PEA, the actions that invite or invoke the PEA are also those that are characteristic of resonant, more effective, and enduring relationships. This tells us that the quality of the relationship between the coach or other helper and the person being coached is key. Working with a coach is not like asking an accountant for help with your taxes. Rather, coaching requires both people to feel safe and open to possibilities.

We have found that three qualities of relationships have this enduring impact on helping others become motivated, learn, and change: shared vision, shared compassion, and shared relational energy. Our close friend and colleague Kylie Rochford has studied various qualities of relationships and finds that these three are essential for both people in a relationship (or all of the people in teams or most people in organizations).[22] Vision gives us hope. Compassion gives us a sense of being cared for and caring for others. Relational energy gives us stamina and perseverance (i.e., grit).

Although invoking the PEA might seem counterintuitive when you are focused on trying to help someone, it is the most effective way to awaken a person's motivation to learn and change. In chapter 5, we will explore in-depth the roles that both PEA and NEA play in the brain, and we'll share insights from our study of the neuroscience behind coaching to the PEA versus the NEA. We also will look at what occurs after invoking someone's PEA: helpers and coaches need to pay attention to the dynamics of what emerges next in the person. This is where balance becomes an issue—between the human instinct to survive and the human desire to thrive.

key learning points

1. Asking someone a positive question awakens the PEA, activating a specific network in the brain that triggers hormones in the *parasympathetic nervous system* (renewal). Asking a negative question or question that pulls a defensive response arouses the NEA, activating a different network in the brain, which triggers hormones in the *sympathetic nervous system* (stress).

2. The PEA is both a state of being open to new ideas *and* a tipping point along the path of sustained, desired change. Coaching with compassion (i.e., coaching to the PEA) serves both purposes.

3. The PEA is being in PNS arousal; feeling positive and hopeful. The NEA is being in SNS arousal; feeling negative and defensive or fearful.

4. Emotions are contagious, both positive and negative emotions. The contagion spreads at fast speeds (often in milliseconds) and is predominantly below conscious awareness.

reflection and application exercise

Over the course of the next week, observe and record your own emotions about three times each day (ideally morning, midday, and evening). Note what you were doing at that particular time, and how you felt in that moment. Avoid listing specifics and instead focus on your emotional state—whether you were feeling happy, angry, sad, excited, or otherwise, or even if you were feeling unsure of your emotional state in that moment. By the end of the week, ideally you will have recorded around twenty entries noting emotional states. Analyze these entries and look for patterns that emerged. What do you notice about your ratio of positive to negative emotions?

conversation guide

1. Discuss with others whether you find yourself at the mercy of negative emotions more than positive emotions. Do you sometimes feel a heavy weight from an internal monologue having to do with negative emotions? Can you override them? What helped?

2. Share with others how much time you spend in an emotionally positive state in your social, professional, and organizational lives. What about the time you spend in an emotionally negative state?

3. Offer observations with others about finding yourself able to move someone else from an emotionally negative state into an emotionally positive one. If so, how did you achieve this? Or did you do the opposite and bring them into a negative state?

4. Discuss with others the most stressful times in your life. What has been the nature of your relationship with those around you, whether at work, home or leisure? Have there been times where you have taken your work home with you, or else dragged stresses and emotional baggage from home into the workplace?

5. Share with others particular things you do or values you hold that you feel have helped you reduce stress or stimulated renewal in your life.

6. Describe to others times in your past or present when you have been the most task-oriented. That is, recall situations where your thoughts have been dominated by problem solving, decision making, and "trying to get things done." Have others ever complained about your behavior in those times? As you look back on those moments, was there anything you missed or didn't enjoy because of your task focus?

survive and thrive

the battle in your brain

Surviving means being able to *live* to function and work. It is not a simple biological process. Survival has emotional and even spiritual dimensions. In the most primal sense, survival means that our bodies continue to function and maintain themselves—breathing, eating, sleeping, and so forth. We make it through another day! Most of us would agree that it seems like a dismal way to live and a boring—if not depressing—way to work. (Of course, it beats the alternative!) And in some coaching situations, we do have to start with simple survival, as we will illustrate later in this chapter.

But in most situations as humans, we aspire to not just survive but also to thrive. We need *both* the PEA and NEA. Snakes, on the other hand, will rely heavily on NEA for survival, while we suspect that the PEA plays only a minimal role, if any, in their lives.[1] But people are different. We need PEA arousal to feel motivated to grow or change, to seek pleasure and to play. As we described in chapter 4, the PEA enables us to thrive by activating stress-alleviating hormones that produce feelings of safety, hope, and even joy. And we need the NEA too, because it helps us survive by activating our stress hormonal response to either fight or make a fast getaway or prepare for a defensive posture in a situation. The NEA also helps us to sharpen our focus cognitively and emotionally, which allows us to perform tasks with mental and physical acuity. When we try to help people as coaches, managers, or other kinds of helpers, we guide them to engage in both the PEA and NEA, and to find the best balance between PEA and NEA at that time in their life and work.

The most effective balance will change over time and depending on the situation, so the coach or manager or teacher should monitor changes in the person's environment and experiences over time. The dilemma is that once a person is in the NEA, she may not "see" a way out and therefore feel stuck. That would block further movement and any self-initiated tipping point into the PEA. Again, the coach or other helper becomes critical to motivating change, learning, and development, which means helping the coachee learn to move back and forth between the PEA and NEA, while staying primarily in the PEA.

In this chapter, we will examine further how this back-and-forth movement can achieve a balance that helps people pursue sustained, desired change. Why? Because the PEA is *both* a tipping point to help someone move to the next stage of change through ICT, *and* the psychophysiological state in which a person is open to new ideas, other people, and emotions. This chapter will also explore in-depth the brain science supporting these ideas, including insights from our study of the neuroscience behind coaching to the PEA versus the NEA. Additionally, we will look at what occurs after invoking someone's PEA—coaches and helpers need to pay attention to the dynamics of what emerges next in the person and help her move ahead. This is where balance becomes an issue, between the human instinct to survive and the human desire to thrive.

coaching to survive

Sometimes when helping someone, we might need to start with simple survival (tapping into the NEA)—such as when an individual has a medical condition or injury that warrants medical attention but is avoiding getting the help they need. There might not be time to examine the underlying causes or help her put it in the context of a long-term vision. She needs help right now. But even coaching someone to survive requires some PEA.[2] Think about it. Even when the person is experiencing symptoms or physical injury, if the coach frames the task of getting medical attention as something she *must or should* do, it might backfire. That is coaching for compliance, which as we've shown invokes the NEA—and for someone not getting medical attention in a timely manner, may trigger other physical problems. That's why even if the NEA is needed initially, it has to be balanced with some PEA to keep the person upbeat and motivated, or in this example, increase the likelihood that she will take the medicine or rehab needed to heal.[3]

Take the situation in which Bob Shaffer found himself.[4] Bob's work as Chief Auditor and Executive Vice President of Fifth Third Bank was challenging and stimulating, and he was doing exceedingly well. But soon after enrolling in a leadership program offered through his employer, he realized he wanted to make some important changes. Working with a coach in the program from Case Western Reserve, Bob reflected on his life balance—specifically, his mind-body-heart-spirit balance, which we contend are the four key components of any process of renewal.[5] Bob concluded: "I'm out of balance on all of them."

Almost twenty years after playing college football and being at the top of his game physically, Bob felt the effects of a career that demanded significant attention and long hours. His life outside of work was also full with family activities that centered around his wife and three daughters. Physical exercise dropped behind personal and professional commitments, and he found himself a hundred pounds over his ideal weight. He could feel how this was depleting his energy and threatening his ability to survive—both as an executive and a person. Although this was both a health problem and a symptom of other challenges he was facing, Bob knew at some point he would have to muster the motivation to lose weight or risk shortening his life and sacrificing time and experiences with the people he loved dearly.

This was a clear invocation of Bob's NEA—the instinct to survive. But the coach knew she would have to invoke the PEA as well if Bob was to have any hope of following through with the changes he knew he had to make. That's why the coach began by asking Bob to develop his vision for his ideal life (and work) ten to fifteen years in the future. As Bob described it, it was the first time in his career where he was asked to focus on "not only my job skills, but more importantly, on my personal development as a leader. It was the first time that I felt it was okay in the workplace to talk about me."

Although Bob knew he wanted a more balanced life in general, he decided to start by committing to improve his physical health. He'd heard about a good personal trainer his friends were using, and he called the trainer the next day. The trainer, like Bob's coach, asked what he wanted to achieve. "I want to live a long healthy life with my wife and three daughters and walk my daughters down the aisle," he said—and added, "I want to run a local 10-K Race." Bob's wife was a runner, and usually he'd wait for her at the finish line of the race. Now he wanted to run the race with her. He said, "I also want to be a positive role model to my family. I want to lose a hundred pounds!"

At this point, Bob joined millions of others around the world. The growth of obesity and evidence of Type II diabetes is an epidemic in both the developed and developing world. But in Bob's case, his need to survive was guided by a clear personal vision and the support of an executive coach and a personal trainer. This changed his prognosis. Bob proceeded to reach some amazing milestones over the next year. He was working out six days a week. He lost 105 pounds and successfully finished the 10-K with his wife. His new energy was evident to his employees and peers at work. He was truly a changed person and it showed. Both his first coach from Case Western Reserve's program who worked with him for a year and another internal coach from within the ranks of Fifth Third Bank who began working with him later were a major source of support for Bob. As he said, "I never had follow-up coaching after an executive program before. It really established the accountability . . . taking the excitement and passion you have in the workshop itself and sustaining it." His coach had stressed the idea of being intentional about change, so Bob regularly committed his intentions to paper. "I'm a big believer in having a personal vision and a personal balance sheet," he said, "and I constantly look at them and refine them."

The sustainable power of invoking the PEA and Bob's vision is evident now, seven years later: he has kept most of the weight off (i.e., a net loss of eighty pounds), he and his wife regularly work out together, and he continues to see his trainer three times a week. Bob still talks about the moments of insight with his coach, and about how developing his personal vision was an exciting tipping point in his life. His transition at work has been equally dramatic. Bob is now Chief Human Resource Officer for the bank, a job he says feels more aligned with his interests and passions—something he felt much more confident to pursue once he'd addressed his health issues and could envision a more positive, hopeful future for himself. He wanted to bring his enthusiasm and increased engagement to the entire bank. In his new role, he is able to put the employee—not compliance—at the center of all of his activities, and those around him respond positively. PEA begets PEA!

Making changes that require self-control is stressful, often depleting our internal reservoir of energy.[6] But sometimes they must be done. "Change is tough, and sustained change is not always a positive experience," says our friend and colleague, Anita Howard. In her coaching and research on coaching, she has become convinced that the NEA is critical to successful transformation and growth.[7] Her father was a prominent minister and head of Washington, DC's, Southern Christian Leadership Conference (SCLC) chapter, and his church was a key staging ground for efforts to promote racial equality in the United States. On many occasions, leaders in the civil rights movement, such as Martin Luther King Jr., Ralph Abernathy, Andrew Young, Jesse Jackson, A. Phillip Randolph, Bayard Rustin, John Lewis, and others would gather in various locations around the country to discuss strategy. Anita was invited to listen from the age of about thirteen. She remembers the feeling of the conversations; for instance, when they were planning the 1963 March on Washington. "What I learned," she said, "was that these people were existentially trapped in NEA landscapes due to the threat and dangers of being black in Jim Crow America—but they were able to tackle the daunting task of social change because they always, always drew on core values and belief. Belief in God, belief in the American Constitution, belief in humanism, belief that all children deserve a better world, whatever their race or tribe. This informed their strategic planning and use of non-violent approaches and methods." So while the NEA played a key role in the meetings Anita witnessed, she says it was the shared vision that provided the context and predominant force for the change efforts to continue.

To understand more about the NEA and how the PEA fits in, let's look at what actually happens in the brain when either of those mechanisms is aroused.

the battle in your brain

A few years ago, the digital industry began talking about the concept of *mindshare*: How much (or what share) of your brain, your conscious brain, are you devoting to a particular thing? The developers of software, mobile apps, and video games, of course, wanted to maximize the share of consumer minds focused on their products. It was another way to ask: What are you paying attention to or focusing on? They were onto something big—that individuals can bring the power of their attention to focus on a particular thing.

The question becomes, then, are you focusing on the right thing? That is what the best coaches guide people to ask themselves. Underlying that question is a growing application of research using neuroimaging and neuroscience to illuminate how our brains actually land on that "right" thing. Our close friend and colleague Anthony Jack has led a team of researchers in his Brain, Mind, Consciousness Lab at Case Western Reserve to further document how our brains use two dominant networks of neurons. He currently thinks it is best to refer to these two networks as the *analytic network* (AN) (historically, the *task positive network*) and the *empathic network* (EN) (historically, the *default mode network*).[8]

Here's how those networks relate to what we've already learned about the PEA and NEA: When a person's PEA is aroused by some kind of positive guidance or experience, his empathic network was activated at the beginning of the experience. And when his NEA is triggered—by negative feedback or discouraging experience—it's the analytic network that was activated at the beginning of the experience.

But there's also a third component that fits into this system, which we learned about in chapter 4: the *renewal system* (technically, the parasympathetic nervous system, PNS) versus the *stress response* (technically, the sympathetic nervous system, SNS). These two states most often go hand in hand, so PNS is usually associated with the EN and SNS is usually associated with the AN. However, they don't always go together. For instance, someone can find himself in a fight-or-flight stress response and experience activation of either his empathic brain (EN) or analytical brain (AN), depending on whether the situation calls for analytic thinking or empathetic thinking and feeling. Likewise, he can be in renewal (PNS) arousal and experience either empathic or analytic activation. In our work, we are most concerned about a specific alignment of a person's inner state. That is, how we can evoke the PEA in ourselves and others by inciting positive (versus negative) feelings while simultaneously activating the EN (versus AN)? We can think of these alignments in terms of equations:

$$PEA = EN + PNS + \text{positive feelings}$$
$$NEA = AN + SNS + \text{negative feelings}$$

Graphically, you can see this described in figure 5-1. In the figure, the psycho-physiological state of being in the PEA is the solid-line oval on the upper-left quadrant. Imagine this in three dimensions: the upper-left quadrant is coming out of the page toward you. This oval also describes how the PEA can be mild (close to the center

helping people change

FIGURE 5-1

Positive (PEA) and negative emotional attractors (NEA) in Intentional Change Theory

Invoking the PEA in the brain is often a threefold process of: (1) inciting positive versus negative feelings; (2) empathic network (EN) versus analytic network (AN) activation; and (3) arousal of the body's parasympathetic (PNS) versus sympathetic nervous system (SNS).

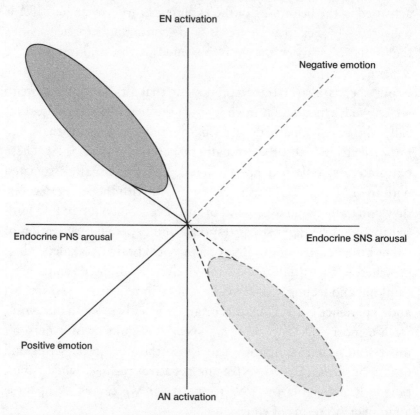

Source: As shown in R. E. Boyatzis, K. Rochford, and S. N. Taylor, "The Role of the Positive Emotional Attractor in Vision and Shared Vision: Toward Effective Leadership, Relationships, and Engagement," *Frontiers in Psychology* 6, article 670 (2015), doi:10.3389/fpsyg.2015.00670.

or tipping point) or intense (toward the outer edge of the oval). Similarly, the state of being in the NEA is "behind the page" three-dimensionally, and in the lower-right quadrant shown by the oval with dotted lines. It is behind the surface of the page moving away from you. This oval also describes how the NEA can be mild (close to the center or tipping point) or intense (toward the outer edge of the oval).

As Anthony Jack's research has repeatedly shown, the important thing for coaches to understand is that the two networks, the analytic and the empathic, have little overlap and are "antagonistic."[9] That is, they suppress each other. If the analytic network lights up for any reason, the person's empathic network gets suppressed, at least in that particular moment—and vice versa. So in our example in chapter 4 of Richard's awkward moment with his wife, he was clearly in the analytic network, which was suppressing his empathic network (and keeping him from noticing his wife).

Both networks play important roles, but in dramatically different ways. We need the AN to solve problems, analyze things, make decisions, and focus (i.e., limit our awareness to direct attention on a task or issue). We need the EN to be open to new ideas, scan the environment for trends or patterns, be open to others and emotions, as well as moral concerns (i.e., truly understanding others' perspectives, not the more analytic activity of making judgments about right and wrong).

For example, when a negative, shocking moment in life strikes— a natural disaster, a heart attack, getting fired, your spouse asking for a divorce—we sometimes call it a "wake-up call."[10] But in fact these things are more likely to predominantly arouse our stress response, and push us into the NEA, where we're unmotivated to create even seriously needed change. Our minds react defensively and begin to close down. As we've described previously, people (some coaches but also managers, parents, doctors, teachers) often try to motivate others by adding more pressure and providing negative feedback. In the process, they induce anxiety and stress in the other person but don't typically motivate change or learning in ways that stick beyond short-term fixes.

And yet there are times when a wake-up call serves as a galvanizing force for change for some people. It occurs when a negative experience is not only shocking but also results in the person taking stock of his values and committing to something meaningful and positive in his life. For example, after a natural disaster, you might have a desire to spend more time with your family. You might realize that responding to another three dozen emails or working a few more hours won't give your life more meaning. If the experience

research spotlight

The research referenced in the endnotes from Anthony Jack and his colleagues shows:

1. When people engage in analytic tasks, like financial, engineering, IT, or physics problems, they activate the analytic network (AN) in their brain. The AN enables a person to focus, solve a problem, and make a decision, and act, but it closes a person perceptually to new ideas, possibilities, and people.

2. When people engage in social tasks in empathic thinking, like helping another person or actively listening to understand, arguing with others, or asking someone for help, they activate the empathic network (EN) in their brain. The EN enables a person to be open to new ideas, people, or emotions and to tune in to others and moral considerations, but might leave a person open to distractions and less immediately prepared to act.

3. The AN and EN are, on the whole, independent networks, and at any given moment they suppress each other. But as professionals, managers, and leaders, we need to use both the AN and EN to be effective. The key is how we cycle between these networks. Balanced oscillation between the networks is associated with high IQ, healthy psychological adjustment, and higher performance.

invokes that kind of positive sense of purpose or a reminder of core values, then the wake-up call has lit up your EN and has converted into a PEA moment, engendering a positive vision of the future.

Note that since both domains are important to our work and life behavior—but they also suppress each other—we believe that effective coaches and other helpers cycle back and forth between addressing the EN and AN.[11] They can do it quickly, likely in under a second. The cycle time may be longer or shorter, depending on the activities involved. We also believe that the best coaches are good at matching a specific situation to the network in a person's brain that they wish to help activate as most appropriate or needed in that situation.

For example, the two domains have been related to different learning styles.[12] People with a preference for abstract conceptualization in their learning process may be activating the AN most often.[13] In contrast, a preference for concrete experience as a learning style is associated with EN activation. We do not know as yet whether more frequent or intense activation of the AN results from training, socialization, or an organization's culture or individual dispositions. For example, the moment between Richard and his wife was but one of many in which he becomes so engrossed in an analytic task that he is virtually blind to the people around him. He attributes this to his years of training as a scientist, first in aeronautics and astronautics and later as a research psychologist—all of which play into his "disposition to be nerdy and analytic," as he says.

The work done in most organizations these days, whether companies or nonprofits, seems to focus on AN activation because of an emphasis on budgets, problem solving, dashboards, metrics, and analytics. We have observed that a person who repeatedly uses her AN—and who is good at it—is given even more analytic assignments. It doesn't take long for a subculture to develop within a department. The people in these clusters begin to see the AN as the most helpful or relevant approach to any situation. They have become a coven of analytics. Another dimension to this preoccupation with one network, in this case the AN and analytics, is that it can lead, in some organizations, to a kind of objectification of people (e.g., referring to people as "human assets to be utilized or maximized").[14]

Because the AN inhibits or limits openness to new ideas, a person being coached to her NEA (e.g., being coached to meet certain job requirements) might give the coach lip service at best. In organizations, such a focus on AN, when combined with a certain pride and esprit de corps in the company, could devolve into

insights from a neuroscience study of coaching

Richard Boyatzis and Anthony Jack at Case Western Reserve University decided to see if they could explain the neural mechanism of the PEA versus NEA experience from coaching.[15] They wanted to see if the parts of the brain and networks they thought related to being more "open" were activated in conversations with a coach invoking PEA experiences, as contrasted with a coach invoking an NEA experience. They had two experienced coaches in their mid-thirties coaching college sophomores (nineteen- and twenty-year-olds). Ten of the subjects in the study were male and ten were female.

Once agreeing to participate in the study, the sophomores had a thirty-minute coaching conversation with one of the two coaches. The next day, they had a conversation with the other coach. One was using a PEA approach to coaching and the other an NEA approach. Which coach did the PEA was determined by a random number table to avoid any implicit bias. Similarly, whether the student received the PEA coaching first or after the NEA coaching was also determined by a random number table.

During the PEA coaching, one question was asked of the student: "If your life was perfect in ten years, what would it be like?" Then the coach asked some clarifying questions. During the thirty minutes of the NEA coaching, four questions were typically asked: "How are you doing in your courses? Are you doing all the assignments? Are you doing all the reading? Are you getting enough time from your instructor?" These were not particularly negative questions, and in fact, many observed that they were the kind of questions their parents or faculty often asked. But the questions were classified as NEA because they typically invoke feelings of guilt, inadequacy, and frustration in students.

After each coaching session, the students confirmed that they saw the person doing the PEA coaching as "inspiring" and "caring." They saw the coach doing the NEA sessions as making them feel "guilty and self-conscious." Three to five days later, each student appeared at the Brain, Mind, Consciousness Laboratory of Professor Jack and was placed into the brain scanner for fMRI (functional magnetic resonance imaging, a method that reveals how different parts of the brain are being activated). Their neural activity was scanned while they were exposed to ninety-six brief (eight- to twelve-second) videos. Each video showed one of the coaches making statements that were inherently PEA, NEA, or neutral. For example, a PEA statement was "As a Case graduate, you will have the tools to contribute positively to your work organization," whereas an NEA statement was "Generally, you have little time for fun while you are here at Case." A neutral statement was, "You are learning at Case."

When the coach who had the PEA session made statements in the video clips that were positive (PEA), several brain regions associated with EN functioning were activated in the students (e.g., the nucleus accumbens, orbitofrontal cortex, and posterior cingulate cortex). When the statements in the videos were made by the coach who did the NEA session and were negative (NEA), some regions of the brain associated with the AN were activated. But the most profound finding was the PEA was strongly associated with activation of the lateral visual cortex, a key brain area involved in imagining things. That means that PEA-based coaching with compassion even for thirty minutes helped to activate brain areas with benefits of being more open to new ideas, change, and learning. Meanwhile, even thirty minutes of NEA-based coaching for compliance tended to activate brain areas that result in narrowed, focused thinking and a defensive experience.

competition neglect, in which key movements in an industry are missed because of inattention to competitors.[16] But at the individual level, it manifests as a reluctance to change and adapt, a reluctance to learn.

Like the PEA and the NEA, we also need both neural networks. If we spend too much time in the EN, we may become distracted and make less progress toward specific goals; if we spend excessive time in the AN, we risk making a moral transgression of some kind. It is not that the person thinks he is doing a "bad" thing, and he typically does know right from wrong, but that he ignores the possibility of something being unfair or unjust because of his focus. For example, he might make decisions that are expedient in terms of budget analysis but still not be best for the organization in the long term. We need the EN to understand things from other people's perspectives and appreciate how a potential decision will impact trust and the relationships.[17]

As a coach (or a manager, teacher, trainer, cleric, or other helper), you want to activate the EN early in the process to help the person become open to new ideas and the possibility of change. It also helps him enter the PEA state, which becomes a tipping point into the five discoveries of sustainable change (Boyatzis's ICT), as described in chapter 3.

For more specifics on coaching to the PEA versus NEA, see the sidebar, "Insights from a Neuroscience Study of Coaching." Also, in chapter 7 we provide further explanation of how to increase the positive quality of one's coaching relationships.

beyond surviving to thriving

If we pursued life as a series of NEA challenges, we might earn points for perseverance and toughness, but the sustainability of change and learning efforts are likely shortened. Life becomes a chore. And we do chores for only as long as we must. So we need to find ways to tap into positive emotions (i.e., PEA and therefore the EN and PNS) as often as possible.

That's what Mary Tuuk has managed to do. Repeated ventures into the PEA have driven her to new heights in life and work. But it wasn't always that way.

When she began working with a coach, Mary (like Bob Shaffer) was a bank executive at a major midwestern bank. As Chief Risk Officer, she had helped steer the company through the turmoil of the financial crisis and the repayment of the Troubled Asset Relief Program (TARP) federal money. Mary's career in risk management was fulfilling—but she knew she wanted something more.

In working with a coach, Mary had the opportunity to contemplate her ideal life and work ten to fifteen years into the future. As she peeled back the layers of others' expectations, traditions, and a siloed career in risk management, she created an exciting image of herself as something else: a line executive responsible for a profit and loss statement (i.e., a general management position). But she also wanted to give more attention to her personal life—she wanted to spend more time singing, and she wanted to visit her aging mother more often. As she discussed these visions with her executive coach, more and more ideas came to her. Being in the PEA was opening her up to new possibilities. Her excitement grew.

When she shared her dream with the CEO, he listened carefully and heard Mary's desire for growth and change at the company. He knew that Mary's law degree and sixteen years in banking had prepared her for a major functional role. He decided to promote her to be president of the bank's affiliate in Grand Rapids, Michigan. He did this while knowing that the responsibility was really at a level for a chief executive. But the CEO thought the job would be a perfect opportunity and challenge for Mary. She would have to leverage and refine her full range of talents.

Fast-forward to one year later, and the results were dramatic. Mary was propelling the bank to new levels of revenue, profit, and growth. As a bank president, she had commercial and retail banking, consumer lending, and investment advisory services reporting to her. She also bought a condo on a lake in western Michigan, which she visited frequently to be close to nature and "recharge her batteries." And she'd found a way to develop and share her love of music and singing: she began to sing regularly with several church choirs. Then, at the local River Run in May 2012, she broke from the stereotypical bank president's role and sang the US national anthem to nearly forty thousand spectators, as well as twenty thousand runners participating in the bank-sponsored community race.

As a Michigan native, Mary soon embraced her new community in western Michigan. She now serves on numerous community boards and sees her role as a community builder. She also works to advance women in business, another priority from her future vision of herself that she developed with her coach, creating a program— the Young Women's Business Institute—at Calvin College in Grand Rapids. Its purpose? To "help young women envision a career in business and dream big," Mary says. The program brings high school students to campus and facilitates social networking with business leaders in the community.

Mary's quest took another turn when her mother became ill and needed her. As she said, "How often do we get a chance to reverse the roles and help our mother?" With her personal vision in mind, she left the bank to spend time with her mother, which was important to both of them. It also enabled Mary to reconnect with her extended family.

Later, Mary took a job at a very different kind of organization: Meijer Inc., a big-box retailer that's a family business, with dramatic growth aspirations across six US states and in Asia. Although her title was initially Chief Compliance Officer, she has now added to it Senior Vice President, Properties and Real Estate. These roles allow her to learn the business and focus on supply chain and suppliers. Mary loves the cross-functional teams in which she can add more value and finds it to be a deeply meaningful role.

Mary has continued her work with internal mentees and her Young Women's Business Institute program, which will have its sixth annual event this year in Michigan. She feels she is living a completely different life from the one she was living before she developed a future vision for herself, having found true meaning in her life. Music is a key part of that, and recently Mary accepted the role as president and CEO of the Grand Rapids Symphony in addition to her regular work for Meijer Inc. Clearly, Mary has gone beyond simple survival, and is truly thriving in her life and at work as the culmination of the work she did to find her ideal self.

achieving the right balance

As Mary's and Bob's stories illustrate, coaches can help people find the best balance between PEA and NEA arousal. That back-and-forth in the brain is critically important. Repeated activation of our NEA results in cognitive, emotional, and perceptual impairment.[18] As research has shown, we need the NEA. But along with the NEA comes arousal of the body's stress response (the sympathetic nervous system, SNS). Even annoying episodes, like someone cutting you off in traffic or your cell phone dropping a call, will activate the SNS. In that moment, you are less creative, experience more difficulty with complex tasks, and reduce your field of vision to a narrow arc (thereby not seeing the people around you and missing a lot of things occurring nearby).[19] Or as one friend—an executive who had a lifelong career in engineering—told us, in the NEA/SNS state, he saw "people as problem-bearing platforms."

For sound ecological reasons, we are designed in such a way that negative emotions are stronger than positive ones.[20] It is difficult to explore flourishing and thriving if you are about to be eaten or die. But once our survival is somewhat established and maybe even ensured for a time, we have a choice: we can live our lives focused on the anticipated negative experiences (what will come up on Facebook or Twitter about me?), or we can move into the PEA.

An ancient Greek philosopher, Kleovoulos, one of the Seven Sages, told us that we should experience things in balance—nothing in excess.[21] Reflect for a moment. When you think of the last time someone said something critical about how you were dressed, did you think about it for a few days, weeks, months? Perhaps it still bothers you. In contrast, when someone said you looked great today, did you continue to think about it for days, weeks, or months? Not likely. How do you achieve balance when negative emotions are stronger?

A creative colleague, Barbara Fredrickson, has developed the *positivity ratio*. She and her colleagues have done dozens of well-designed research studies to show that having more positive than negative feelings is good for a person's functioning at work and at home. An early part of her work suggested a desirable ratio of 3:1 in teams. The mathematics of that article came under criticism but did not threaten the soundness of being more positive than negative. Her subsequent studies showed how a great positivity ratio leads to better health (a better-functioning immune system), better cognitive performance, and better social experiences.[22]

In the intimate arena of marriage, John Gottman and his colleagues spent more than fifty years studying loving, stable couples. They found that a 5:1 PEA-to-NEA ratio is needed if a marriage is to thrive. For those of us who are married, that is a challenging target![23]

In another fMRI study about the impact of PEA versus NEA coaching, we looked at how much PEA would be sufficient to clearly activate the PNS and renewal systems.[24] We discovered that two PEA coaching sessions to one NEA-based session significantly activated the ventral medial prefrontal cortex, which is the part of the brain that directly activates the PNS.[25]

Of course, the specific ratio to achieve a desired balance would depend on a person's current state, mood, and events happening in life and at work. While some claim work-life balance (or work-family balance) is a crucial goal, we believe it is more of an aspiration. No one ever gets there, but it is important to keep it in mind and continue to rebalance your activities and use of energy and time. Coaching to the PEA can help, whether you're the person being coached or the coach/helper.

We need the PEA more often than we think. Most of us tolerate negative environments and relationships—sadly, we have come to expect them. Research on states described by the PEA and NEA suggests that, for sustainable change, a person needs to be in the PEA two to five times the frequency or amount of time as in the NEA.[26]

For example, when using data-based feedback—like 360 assessment results—showing a person the data, graphs, or report will typically result in his focusing on the gaps, weaknesses, or negative comments. This likely activates the AN as he tries to analyze it, and the NEA as he reacts in a defensive manner. At this point in the process, he is becoming increasingly closed to new possibilities. While he may admit the importance of using the feedback, the sustainability of any effort is diminished because of the stress and strain it adds.

On the other hand, if he focuses on his personal vision *before* he hears any feedback (e.g., 360-degree assessments), he has a greater chance of creating a positive, strongly desired context for the feedback. That is, the context should be his vision and dreams. Our close friends and colleagues at ESADE in Barcelona, professors Leticia Mosteo, Joan Manuel Batista, and Ricard Serlavos, have shown that twenty-five- to thirty-five-year-old MBAs improve their personal vision dramatically, as well as their emotional and social intelligence behavior, as a result of a course focused on their personal vision versus other more traditional approaches of focusing on correcting weaknesses that appear from feedback of various sources, including their 360-degree feedback.[27] But even in helping individuals make sense of 360 feedback, the coach first should focus on the person's strengths to further emphasize the PEA state and keep it going as long as possible. Then discussing the weaknesses or gaps in the context of one's dream and vision as well as strengths becomes a useful aspect of the AN.

renewal and stress

As we've shown, when coaching someone to sustainable change, the coach—or manager, teacher, parent, cleric, doctor—must manage the person's balance between PEA and NEA. This includes a subtler juggle: managing the balance of stress and counter-stress, or renewal. As with PEA and NEA, the desire is to have frequent cycling between the two experiences. The body's stress response (SNS) is part of the NEA, and the body's renewal (PNS) is part of the PEA. We need stress not just to survive, but also to help us focus and narrow our vision when needed. The dilemma is that in today's world, we are dosed with too much stress. Often the stresses are minor, but they are persistent and in huge quantities. We forget that this morning was our turn for the car pool, or we miss an email about a change of meeting times, and on and on. When this is added with the occasional acute stress of a major problem at work or home, it tips us into the realm of chronic stress and strain—which is bad for us and those around us.

Coaches, managers, and other helpers can guide people to balance stress and renewal during the coaching process, but they also need to prepare people to handle that balance themselves in daily life. Both Mary and Bob were able to develop new, sustainable habits of renewal with the help of a coach. They learned to prepare for inevitable moments of stress, but also to give themselves the antidote to stressful experiences through activities of renewal—for example, meditation, modest exercise, yoga, prayer to a loving God, being hopeful about the future, being with someone you love, taking care of those less fortunate or the elderly, playing with a pet dog or cat, laughing and being playful, and a walk in nature.[28] Those are the kinds of experiences or activities that can flip a switch in our bodies, call for the PNS and hopefully the PEA.

Most of us know when we are feeling annoyed, frustrated, angry, hurt, or any of the correlates of a stress-induced, or SNS, experience. But fewer of us know how it feels to be in a renewal moment, since it is easily confused with rest, relaxation, or boredom. That is where mindfulness practices can help (see chapter 7 about being present and attentive with others). Training ourselves to recognize moments of renewal when we see or feel them (watching the sunset on the horizon, petting a dog), and then allowing ourselves to become present for them, helps us maintain that all-important balance between stress and renewal. So does variety and change.

variety is more than the spice of life

One reason Bob Shaffer had become unhealthily overweight and out of shape was because, over the years, he'd developed habits that turned his stress into serious conditions that created even more stress. Eating fast food because we don't have time to get groceries and prepare and sit down for a meal is an example of a habit many people can relate to. Also, the quality of the food that we do consume plays a role in the nutritional value of what fuels our bodies. Overeating is often a response to stress. We seek the comfort of the fullness of our stomachs and pleasure of certain tastes or textures. Sometimes the process of eating is distracting and provides a moment of relief from the things haunting us.

Any addiction follows a similar path. Abusive drinking has been shown to result from feeling relatively powerless.[29] We seek relief and relaxation from a drink. Sometimes, we seek further relaxation and have two or three drinks. Once we develop a habit of having a few drinks whenever we feel stressed, it becomes associated with other sensations. Former cigarette smokers often report that they still feel the urge to smoke after dinner or with coffee. This is acknowledgment of a habituation, or addiction. It may start as a behavioral addiction—the action helps us. With time, when chemical substances like caffeine, cigarettes, or alcohol are involved, we begin to experience psycho-physiological changes. Now the habit is more than a pleasant moment. We come to expect it and then need it.

Whether a person is battling an addiction or merely trying to improve performance, substituting one less effective or even bad habit for another habit is a major mistake. It recreates the conditions that the person is trying to change. In addiction treatment circles, we call it *exchanging addictions*.

Variety, it turns out, really helps. To combat annoying or chronic stress, being comfortable with using a variety of renewal activities is a potent antidote.[30] Bob Shaffer succeeded in sustaining his changes because he engaged in renewal moments through consistent and modest physical exercise, competing in events with his wife that were fun, like running, changing his eating habits and routines, and even changing how he approached his work. Mary Tuuk did the same. She engaged in things like building relationships with the bank's community, singing, teaching women to make positive career moves, and spending time with her mother and friends.

So variety is important, but so is dosage. Pharmaceutical companies worry about dosage. Our doctors worry about the correct or best dosage. The same applies to renewal activities. For example, studies show that if you were to spend sixty minutes working out as a renewal activity in a day, your battle to reverse the effects of stress would be better suited by breaking that into four separate fifteen-minute activities.[31] For example, fifteen minutes of talking with friends about their lives; fifteen minutes of a breathing or meditation or yoga exercise; fifteen minutes of playing with your children or dog (or cat); and fifteen minutes of joking and laughing with friends or family. Of course, we are not saying you should not exercise. (And truly, you need more than sixty minutes of renewal in a typical day and spread out throughout the week.) But it's a good example of how smaller doses, in terms of time and more frequent episodes of renewal activities, are better than longer, less frequent ones. And using a variety of activities in renewal is better than using the same one or two repeatedly.

Now that we have explained the basic processes going on in the body and mind, we can be more specific about what a coach or helper can do to bring a person more frequently into the PEA. In chapter 6, we will explore how creating a positive context for your future—a personal dream and vision—can help to sustain learning and change.

key learning points

1. To sustain a change or learning process, a person needs to regularly cycle into the PEA two to five times more often than being in the NEA.

2. Renewal activities in smaller doses in terms of time and more frequent episodes of renewal activities are better than longer, less frequent ones.

3. Renewal using a variety of activities is better than using the same one or two repeatedly.

4. The PEA enables us to thrive by activating renewing, stress-alleviating hormones that produce feelings of safety, hope, and even joy. The NEA helps us survive by activating our stress hormonal response to a threat, namely fight, flight, or freeze.

5. Our brains use two dominant networks of neurons regarding learning and change: the *analytic network* (AN) and the *empathic network* (EN). We need the AN to solve problems, analyze things, make decisions, and focus. We need the EN to be open to new ideas, scan the environment for trends or patterns, and be open to others and their emotions, as well as moral concerns. We need both of these networks. Because they are antagonistic and suppress each other, we need to balance time spent in each one.

reflection and application exercise

Go back to the exercise in chapter 4. What NEA experiences or activities can you avoid, minimize, or eliminate in your life and work? What PEA activities or experiences can you do more of during each week, either more frequently or for a longer duration? If you had the time, what new and different PEA activities or experiences would you try to add?

conversation guide

1. Discuss with friends or colleagues how most people do not feel as if they have the best work-life balance. How are people's experiences the same or different? How can you move closer

to a desired balance? What would others around you say about your ability to manage this balance?

2. After reviewing each day from last week, describe to others how many PEA and NEA moments you had each day. Do you or they see any patterns in the observations?

3. In the above discussion, explore which renewal activities you used typically each week and when? How many of the PEA or NEA moments lasted more than fifteen minutes? Which renewal activities could you add to your day or week that would require minimal disruption of current activities or obligations?

the power of a personal vision

dreams, not just goals

A clear and compelling personal vision can transform your life. In 2013, Diana Nyad, at age sixty-four, became the first person confirmed to swim the 103 miles from Cuba to Florida. It was her fifth and final attempt; she had had to terminate four previous crossings since her first try in 1978. In an interview on CNN after her historic achievement, she described her motivation: thirty-five years before, she'd had a dream to do the swim—something that no one had ever done before—and each time, something prevented her from reaching her goal.

"But you move on with life," she said, "and you turn sixty, and your mom dies, and you're looking for something. And the dream comes waking out of your imagination."[1]

Dreams that are connected to values we hold dear, our deepest passions and purpose in life, are always there. They might take a back seat to duties and responsibilities in life, shoved into a metaphorical closet for years. But they don't ever really die. What fueled Diana Nyad's incredible ambition, fortitude, and resilience were the seeds of an exciting dream, planted in her twenties, that carried personal meaning and fulfilled a deep purpose for her well into her sixties.

Helping people identify their personal vision (what we call *coaching to vision*) allows them to remember their long-held dreams and provides a platform from which they can take flight and become reality. We know from sports psychology research, meditation, and biofeedback that we can engage emotional commitment if we can give life to our dreams. A compelling personal vision transforms purpose into action, makes order out of chaos, instills confidence, and drives us to fulfill a desired future.

Throughout this book, we've described how uncovering such a vision unleashes positive emotion in individuals as well as within the coaching relationship itself (or any relationship in which one person is trying to help another). It's so powerful and important that it's essential for guiding people to think more openly and deeply, to connect with who they are authentically at their core, and to ultimately foster learning and change that is lasting. With this chapter, we will explore the personal vision in-depth and discuss ways to help people tap into it. We'll describe research showing that discovery and development of such a vision is the most powerful way—neurologically and emotionally—to engage the PEA and help a person open up to possibilities in life and work. But first let's look at what a personal vision is—and isn't.

dreams, not just goals

A person's vision is her image of a possible future. It is not a goal or a strategy. It consists of neither actions nor obligations. It is not a forecast of what is likely. It is a dream! While coaching for performance emphasizes feedback as an intervention, vision-based coaching emphasizes discovery and expression of the coachee's ideal self as an anchor for the engagement or relationship. The ideal self gives shape and color to what's desired and needed for the person to be at her best.

Put simply, a personal vision is an expression of an individual's ideal self and ideal future. It encompasses dreams, values, passions, purpose, sense of calling, and core identity.[2] It represents not just what a person desires to *do*, but also who she wishes to *be*.

Thinking about any one aspect of a personal vision can sometimes be a completely new or even uncomfortable experience initially because the invitation to introspection may represent foreign territory. Throughout our lives, we are mostly asked what we want to do and not about the kind of person we aspire to be or what kind of life we wish to lead. This starts playfully with toddlers and preschoolers, who are asked, "What do you want to do when you're bigger?" by well-meaning parents, caregivers, and teachers. Children have fun dressing up in costumes to look and act like the person they might want to be when they grow up—a doctor, a firefighter, a ballerina, a nurse, police officer, and the like.

As children get older, they read about different careers, go on field trips, and listen to friends' parents talk about what their jobs involve. All of these experiences help them begin to discover what they might want to do in life. In high school, students are often asked, "Where do you want to go to college?" Then in college, we're coached to answer the interviewer's inevitable question, "What do you want to do after graduation?" Later, in organizations, well-intentioned superiors and human resource managers ask employees, "What would you like to do here in the next several years?"

Clearly, then, we get a lot of practice answering questions about what we want to *do*—but tend to spend a lot less time asking ourselves a question that we think is equally or maybe even more important: "Who do I wish to *be*?" When we as coaches (or parents, teachers, managers, clerics) ask people to consider what they care deeply about, what they dream about, what they think about when they don't have to be thinking about something else, a floodgate of new ideas and possibilities often emerge and flow. And while most organizations focus on career goals two to three years out, we advocate that people think in terms of ten to fifteen years in the future. Why? Because a longer time horizon pushes people past the comfort zone of simply responding with their most recent thought or idea or what's socially expected or accepted. So we ask, "If your life were *ideal* (you could substitute *incredible, amazing, awesome,* etc., here) ten to fifteen years from now, what would it be like?" The initial response to that question can range from a blank stare to a look of anxiety to an expression of pure enthusiasm. But regardless of the response in the moment, the question often eventually results in a smile as the person envisions himself authentically in the distant future and free from immediate concerns.[3] Such a response taps into his PEA and allows for far more creative ideas and solutions to emerge than he might have had otherwise.

Karen Milley experienced this firsthand. When she participated in a leadership development program at Case Western Reserve University, Karen was a vice president of research and development. One homework assignment was to practice drawing out vision in other people. She chose to practice first with her teenage son, John, one evening as they sat around their fire pit. "Tell me what you want to be," she asked, "and what you see yourself doing in fifteen years." He paused, then said, "That question requires me to imagine."

That's when a light bulb went on for Karen. "That is the power of coaching to vision," she thought. "It requires people to imagine!"

When she recounted the story, she added that at her company, people are used to thinking in terms of "What role are you going after?" She said, "Everyone feels like they need a well-thought-out, five-year plan, ready to pull out of their drawer when asked. You stumble because you want to be impressive. But when you ask people to think much further out, you get way past *next* to what do I want to do *last*?" As a leader of a large division, Karen found this refreshing and exciting; and by using the longer timeframe, she immediately noticed a positive shift in thinking and energy in the people she managed.

"Today I give people permission to have two or three scenarios of a possible future," she said, "and I assure them that we'll work with those and figure out the path that's best for them. You can see them light up—they are able to relax and settle down emotionally."

We think Lewis Carroll best suggested the problem of *not* having a personal vision in *Alice's Adventures in Wonderland* when Alice came to a fork in the road, saw the Cheshire Cat in a tree, and asked: "'Would you tell me, please, which way I ought to go from here?' 'That depends a good deal on where you want to get to,' said the Cat. 'I don't much care where—,' said Alice. 'Then it doesn't matter,' said the Cat.'"[4]

But in reality, knowing where we want to go often *does* matter. Developing a picture of where we'd like to go—in our career, in our relationships, in our life—serves as a compass, pointing us toward our destination; it allows us to see various routes to travel versus just one and keeps us on the best path to reach it. That's why it's important to start the coaching process by exploring a person's ideal self and translating that into an outward expression of some sort, often a written statement or an image. The process of unearthing and distilling a personal vision unleashes powerful positive energy and holds many benefits. It helps us to see a bigger picture, engage in intelligent thought, be more empathetic, move to action, enact a larger range of behaviors, and build resilience to get through the tough times. (See the sidebar "Healing and the Personal Vision" for a story from one of this book's authors, Ellen, on using these tools to address a health crisis.)

Our good friend and colleague Angela Passarelli examined what happens cognitively, emotionally, physiologically, and relationally during contrasting coaching conversations anchored in the PEA and the NEA. Participants in her study met with two coaches who engaged them in different ways. One coach asked the participants to envision a positive future (PEA) and the other encouraged the individuals to focus on current problems (NEA), both in service of helping the participants advance their careers. Participants' experience with the two coaches was notably different. After the vision-based coaching, they felt happier, reported a higher perceived quality of the coaching relationship and expressed more aspirational goals. Participants were also willing to exert significantly more effort to pursue goals set after the PEA-based coaching session than after the NEA-based session, and they found more joy in pursuing them.[5]

healing and the personal vision

It was November 2004 and Ellen was in the first semester of her PhD program. Sitting in class one day, she felt a lump on the side of her neck. She didn't remember having felt it before and dismissed it as a sign that she was just fighting an oncoming cold. But when it didn't go away after a week, she made an appointment to see her doctor. After multiple doctors' visits, lab work, and a biopsy, she received the kind of news no one ever wants to hear: she had a rare form of salivary gland cancer. Fortunately, the cancer was caught early and she had the gland surgically removed, followed by radiation. Still, she'd been completely blindsided by the diagnosis, and as a mother (her daughter was almost four at the time), she knew she needed to do everything possible to improve her prognosis. On top of caring for her daughter and studying in her doctoral program, she was also working full-time. Her husband had just purchased a medical clinic, so the family needed her income to stay afloat. There was a lot on her plate. This was her wakeup call that something had to change, and she had no choice but to listen to it.

At the time, Ellen was already an experienced coach and she was well versed in the Intentional Change Theory (ICT) (described in chapter 3). She decided to apply the model and began by developing her personal vision for her life post-diagnosis. She got in touch with her core values—faith, family, friendship, love, health, integrity, lifelong learning, and fun—and what she truly wanted in her future.

Ellen immediately felt the power of developing her vision, of clarifying what really mattered to her and the legacy that she wanted to leave in her life. That clarity gave her the energy and strength to apply the third discovery of the ICT, which is to put together goals and the actions she needed to take for her future well-being, and then do everything possible to follow the plan. She began by taking a medical leave from school to allow herself to heal—not without a lot of angst, since she had only just begun her program. She developed a close "coaching" relationship with a Catholic nun who had been a former teacher in high school and who offered her spiritual direction. They met monthly for a year, often discussing how scripture passages were relevant to her life experience and the role of faith and grace in her trial.

In parallel with radiation treatments, Ellen opened her mind to learn about how to be healthy holistically. She worked with a naturopathic doctor on a process of nutritional detoxification and learned about the power of food as medicine. She transformed her diet to significantly decrease white, refined sugar and increase the amount of organic foods, whole foods, and vegetables she consumed. Smoothies made with a green drink mixture and other ingredients became her daily staple in order to amplify her intake of high-quality nutrients. She learned transcendental meditation from a well-known Ayurvedic doctor. She exercised several times a week. She listened to audio CDs of guided imagery to direct her thoughts to work in conjunction with, rather than against, her body to calm her mind when it went into overdrive worrying about the "what-ifs" and to remain hopeful instead of afraid and depressed. Being intentional about living out her vision and values took every ounce of energy she had. And she "followed this plan with the help of many supportive family, friends, and colleagues. She joked that it took a village to get her healthy and that the villagers were working overtime.

That was fifteen years ago, and Ellen remains grateful for the gift of a healthy life every day since. She reflects on the experience as life-changing and incredibly empowering. As she puts it,

> In addition to following the advice of my doctors and completing conventional cancer treatments, I made it my personal mission to learn everything that I could from doctors, health professionals, and spiritual advisers who had a teachable point of view on how to live a long, healthy life in the long term and to heal from

cancer in the short term. My main motivation was to not just survive the cancer diagnosis but to be as vibrantly healthy as I could be. I learned that meant striving to be exceptionally healthy and well mentally, emotionally, and spiritually, not just physically. Ultimately, it was so meaningful that even though all of the steps I took seemed crazy to some, I really didn't care what anyone thought about what I was doing because I had nothing to lose and everything to gain. It was liberating.

What's more, Ellen viewed her journey as the ultimate test of ICT. "It was very clarifying for me to stare death in the face and get crystal clear on what my values were and what I deeply desired," she says. "It wasn't working more hours every day and collapsing into bed exhausted. It was a deeper desire to live out God's plan for my life, connect with who I really was, be with the people who I cared for, and do work that truly helped people and organizations. Only from that place did I have a chance at healing."

As beneficial and worthwhile as having a personal vision can be, sometimes the process of discovery isn't straightforward or smooth. Take Amy Szabo, for example. It wasn't so much that she didn't know where she wanted to go. Rather, she was interested in so many different paths that it took her some time to develop a personal vision that could allow her to focus on her heart's desire.

amy's story

She got there just in time. Running with her jump bag, Amy Szabo stabilized another heart attack victim and got him to the hospital.

research spotlight

Researcher Angela Passarelli examined how coaches help others manifest lasting change by conducting an experiment looking at the physiological, cognitive, emotional, and relational mechanisms that exist during contrasting coaching conditions. Forty-eight graduate students participated in two distinctly different coaching conversations: one focused on helping the student to imagine the future (the PEA condition) and another focused on existing problems and challenges (the NEA condition). Passarelli collected data during and between the two coaching conversations.

Compared with coaching that focused on current problems, vision-based coaching (coaching that emphasizes the PEA) left participants feeling more uplifted emotionally, reporting a higher-quality relationship with their coach and setting a higher number of goals. The goals that participants set were considered deeply important, and individuals indicated more willingness to exert effort to pursue them, despite considering the goals to be as difficult as goals set in the other coaching condition.

Source: A. M. Passarelli, "Vision-Based Coaching: Optimizing Resources for Leader Development," Frontiers in Psychology 6 (2015): 412, doi:10.3389/fpsyg.2015.00412.

Today, when Amy talks about her early career as an emergency medical technician (EMT), her enthusiasm about helping people comes through. Before becoming an EMT, she'd earned her BS in education and worked briefly as a teacher and then a firefighter—one of two full-time women among 150 men.

Later, after her years as an EMT, she earned a second bachelor's degree, this time in nursing. Before long, she became a clinical nurse manager and the Continuous Improvement Facilitator for the critical care and medical surgical value streams. When she noticed inefficiencies in what she saw at the hospital, she studied to become a Six Sigma Black Belt in Lean Processes. Heads of other units often asked for her help and perspective. Amy was then hired in a different hospital system to help develop a patient experience program alongside chief officers.

Clearly, teacher to firefighter to nurse to hospital patient experience manager is not a typical career path. Amy has gone from saving lives one at a time to saving entire hospitals. Along the road, she's found unique ways to engage in her work, proving herself in each job against any set standard of physical stamina, technical knowledge, and speed. But looking back, she admits that rather than having a plan, she often picked her next steps one at a time, based on things other people had suggested, and testing them as she experienced them.

Fast forward—now in the middle of an executive MBA program, Amy is excited about future possibilities, but uncertain as to which path to choose. She is sure of one thing, however: her former way of choosing careers was an inefficient and ineffective way to move ahead in her life.

A leadership coach in the program worked with Amy to develop a personal vision. "If your life were perfect in ten to fifteen years," he asked her, "what would it be like?" Amy said she hadn't previously given much thought to her long-term future. Indeed, Amy came across as a humble, gentle person, ready to help others rather than focus on herself. Her coach wasn't surprised, therefore, that in her first attempt at crafting a personal vision, Amy centered on her family and on creating more positive environments in health care—not on her own long-term dreams.

The coach decided to continue on for the moment and worked with Amy to decode a multi-rater feedback instrument, the Emotional and Social Competence Inventory (ESCI).[6] Most ESCI users aspire to get eight to ten people to complete the 360-degree feedback survey, and they often have to settle for fewer responses. Not Amy! She set a new record. She solicited fifty people to answer questions about their interactions with her, and forty-seven of them did it.

Later, she reviewed the feedback with her coach. Aside from the incredible response rate, the greatest shock to Amy was the undeniable message in the data from those forty-seven people: Amy consistently demonstrated every emotional, social, and cognitive intelligence competency above the threshold level of "distinctive strengths." She was a resonant leader with high emotional and social intelligence—and she hadn't even known it.

When her coach asked Amy what sense she made of the results, she hesitantly admitted that she was pretty good at leading others. She'd begun to believe, too, that she was ready for a long-term view of her life and not merely the next job. This began another round of personal discoveries for Amy, and she returned to her work at the hospital with a new openness to discovering and seeking her dream future.

When she sat with her coach again six months later, however, Amy admitted to feeling a little lost. She'd had another promotion with more responsibility—a chance to create yet another innovative, new center at the hospital focused on reorienting the entire system or, more accurately, sets of systems in a large health-care faculty around effective and efficient patient care.

Her coach asked if her vision had changed in the months since they had last discussed it. It had. Amy had begun to see herself as a leader and someone others valued as a source of help. She had tackled new challenges and made it a priority to help other hospitals seeking her advice on starting similar initiatives. She'd even begun teaching seminars on emotional intelligence as a way to bring others along in creating high-impact, positive patient-care experiences.

The coach asked her the same question he'd asked earlier that year: "If your life were perfect in ten to fifteen years, what would it be like?" He wondered if she might want to be a president or managing director of a hospital. But she surprised him by leaning forward and excitedly reporting what she would love most: helping hospital leaders see how their behavior affected others and exploring with them better ways to interact with staff and patients. Amy wanted to be a coach for health-care executives.

"Aren't you already doing that?" the coach asked. Amy looked at him with a puzzled smile and said, "What do you mean?"

"Well," he said, "you regularly have conversations now with a wide variety of leaders in your hospital about their units, their behavior, and style."

"Yes," Amy said. "But I am not their coach."

"Are you sure?" he replied.

She thought a minute. "You know, one of the hospital directors called me recently and said that some conversations I'd had with her had been very helpful. She wanted to continue them. I guess that could be the start of a coaching relationship." Amy then asked her coach how she could further develop her skills through advanced training and education in coaching.

Today, when she talks about her dream of coaching and running a major department at the large hospital system where she works, she leans in, smiles, and talks fast. Her energy is infectious. Amy will soon complete her training as a coach—something she credits her own leadership coach for helping her to begin. By guiding Amy to think ahead and construct a comprehensive personal vision, she developed a holistic map for her career and life that she describes as "liberating." Now she wants to help others do the same thing.

Next, we'll look at another individual whose personal vision led to growth and change—at several different points during his career.

bassam's story

Bassam was becoming more and more frustrated with others in the project teams on which he worked in the health-care industry. When he was project leader, he realized that he was aggressive and impatient. It was an odd feeling. He'd always been the nice guy to whom people talked about a wide range of problems and issues. Now it was as if some alien species from another planet had invaded his body and he was the nemesis of the person he'd once been.

He decided he needed a tune-up on his vision and his plan for moving toward it. A year before, in an MBA program, Bassam had worked with a coach and developed a personal vision. He had learned a great deal about himself through that experience and thought working with a coach again might be a good idea since he now faced a different puzzle. Although he was moving along on his career in health care, he wanted something more. Originally from Jordan, Bassam had lived in Dubai for years but had hoped to change his leadership style to become more effective, even charismatic, by gaining international experience and an MBA.

Once again he met with a coach, who asked him about his vision. Bassam described a thoughtful and compelling dream that included maintaining his friendships and being an authentic, friendly person, whom others saw as caring and nice. The coach asked, "So what is the issue?" Bassam explained that in his eagerness to innovate and solve organizational problems, he was often in or leading special project teams. Some team members didn't take their work seriously and weren't very engaged, doing the bare minimum. Social loafing, or freeloading, is a common complaint in project teams, and it made Bassam angry. It did not take long in the new teams for others to see him as the angry task manager—not the caring and innovative leader he wished to be.

The coach asked Bassam where he wanted to be on this apparent continuum between frustrated taskmaster and caring team leader. He said that although being innovative and achieving goals was a part of his personal dream as an effective leader, being seen as an angry person and losing friendships as a result were not a part of his ideal self. This clarification of his vision meant that he needed to adjust some of his behavior.

The coach pressed him around what he thought of the apparent tension in his personal vision. Bassam's answer was quick and clear: he didn't want to achieve team goals at the expense of his relationships.

"Before your team meetings," asked the coach, "are you aware of your growing frustration?"

Bassam said he was, but didn't know what to do about it.

"If you did know what to do," the coach asked, "what would you do?"

Bassam thought for a minute. "I could just ignore the freeloaders and move on with the others who care!" he said smiling, only half-joking. Then, he grew more serious. "I'm not sure what else to do."

The coach invited him to brainstorm and several ideas emerged. Before team meetings, Bassam could take a few minutes to review his vision, even recite it out loud, and reflect on its relevance to the team project. "Reflect on your core values and personal purpose," he encouraged, "and imagine how you want to show up with the team. At the beginning of each meeting, help the team to remember their shared values and vision."

"Focus on the purpose shared by the group," the coach continued, "and acknowledge the efforts of those helping to contribute to the overall outcome. Invite others to reflect and share what they are excited about. In essence, shift the focus to the great progress of the team and let the team share in the need to bring the others along."

This was a shift in thinking for Bassam. He felt relieved at the idea that he alone didn't need to carry the burden of the team's work. Then the coach helped him consider different approaches he might take with the team that would enable him to stay true to how he wanted others to experience him and contribute in significant ways to the team's productivity.

Like Bassam, we all need to update our personal vision on a regular basis. Events may occur that precipitate a change or at least, a reexamination of one's vision, like getting fired or a major promotion, getting married, having a child, losing a parent, or experiencing a natural disaster like a hurricane or a terrorist attack. Sometimes it is not the setting but the people around you who change. Sometimes, however, it isn't an event but the effect of the passage of time.

We all can expect transitions in life and jobs, and those changes can remind us to update our vision. Richard has begun a series of studies with Udayan Dhar on how a person's ideal self or personal vision changes over time and events throughout life.[7] But even without specific events, Richard and Udayan found in an earlier

study that our lives and careers seem to rotate through cycles lasting five to nine years (with an average of seven years). Often, in our
forties and fifties, these are labeled midlife crises, but they really
are a natural rhythm of life and work.[8] It's important for people
to use these natural cycles (or when major events transpire in their
lives) to reexamine their personal vision.

how a personal vision creates change: more evidence

It took us years to understand why there was such a difference in
an individual's response between listing "goals" and discussing a
personal vision, as Amy and Bassam did with their coaches. Goals
ask people to declare something to which they aspire and are sup-
posed to achieve. For many people (other than those with a motive
called a *high need for achievement*, such as people who seek a
career in sales), this creates an obligation.[9] The obligation creates
stress and begins to add to the negative process in the brain that
we've described throughout this book. The goal then may become
something to avoid rather than pursue.

And yet, in earlier research in psychology and management (conducted by Richard and others), we found that goals are helpful but
differ in usefulness based on the situation. The difference lies in
whether the context is performance oriented or learning oriented.
A performance orientation emphasizes a demonstration of competence in pursuit of external recognition and achieving specific
goals. A learning orientation is characterized by a desire to acquire
deep knowledge and skill mastery to apply to a variety of current
and potential scenarios.[10] Other well-established research suggests
that setting specific performance or learning goals leads to different
outcomes. When a task is complex and requires learning and adaptation, learning goals lead to better performance. Participants stay
engaged with the task longer. When the task is simple or routine by
comparison, performance goals motivate greater performance by
providing direction and clarity.[11]

Emerging social neuroscience research helps us to understand the dynamic of why this occurs. When we set a goal, we begin to think of how to work toward it. This invokes the analytical brain. As we first discussed in chapter 5, parts of this network invoke our stress response and often impair us cognitively, emotionally, and physically. By focusing on the goal, we tend to see what is directly in front of us and lose sight of other possibilities on the horizon.[12] Researcher Tory Higgins offers that setting a specific target shifts our focus into preventing the possibility of missing the goal (that is, a preoccupation with achieving the goal itself)—rather than searching for a new possibility altogether.[13] His work shows how this impacts the way we regulate and engage our perceptions. A prevention focus makes us feel slightly to highly defensive—and that limits how we can draw on the internal energy required to initiate something new as well as sustain our efforts toward it. An example that many of us can relate to is the practice of setting a New Year's resolution. With the promise of a brand-new year and a clean slate, we enthusiastically declare a commitment to eat better, get more sleep, call our mother every day, go to church every Sunday, or correct certain bad habits once and for all—only to lose steam after a few weeks. Just ask fitness club managers who love the month of January when people sign up, pay their dues for months or more, and then stop showing up by March. This is because change is difficult, and for adults to change in ways that *stick*, the desire has to run deep. It has to connect to our passion, our purpose, and our core values.

As we saw with Amy Szabo, she started out her career wanting a job (teaching), then an exciting job (firefighting and being an EMT), then a job in which she could focus on helping people (nursing and hospital administration). As her dreams for the future expanded and crystallized, she became more confident in the idea that the dream could become reality—and in her ability to manifest it. It became her personal vision with a deep sense of purpose.

In an interesting twist, we discovered in one of our fMRI studies of coaching that writing one's vision did not activate the same neural networks as *talking* about it with a coach trained in evoking the PEA.[14] As we discussed in an earlier chapter, results from two fMRI studies conducted on PEA-based versus NEA-based coaching showed the power of coaching to one's vision.[15] In the first study, we found that PEA-based coaching to vision activated the portion of the brain most associated with imagining. In the second, we showed that coaching to the PEA, again even for just thirty minutes, activated a person's global focus and ability to see the big picture—versus the NEA, which activated a much more limited local focus.

All of which is to say that discovering one's personal vision—essentially, an ideal vision of one's self and one's future—unleashes positive emotions of hope and excitement that in turn, propels our motivation and appetite for growth and change. Suddenly, we believe that something worthwhile and desirable is going to happen.[16] And that hope is propelled by self-efficacy—a belief in our ability to manifest what we set out to do or be—and optimism. So, hope fueled by self-efficacy means that we not only imagine that good things are about to happen, but we also believe in our ability to achieve them.[17]

In a study of engineering and science professionals focused on why women leave or stay in the field, researchers Kathleen Buse and Diana Bilimoria found empirical evidence for the power of having a vision as a way to equip women in technical fields to develop self-efficacy. For these women, taking the time to reflect upon their passion, purpose, and values increased their engagement in work and strengthened their commitment to a career in engineering.[18]

That was certainly the case for Brandi DiMarco, who worked in information systems at a food-processing manufacturer. While attending a leadership development program, Brandi created a personal vision with the help of an executive coach. She shared the following reflection:

> Having a personal vision helps me to prioritize and prepare for the future. I often go back to my notes and read what I wrote. My vision and values are hung by my mirror, so I look at them every day to remind myself of who I really am. It's easy to forget when life happens. Personally, I've decided to have another child . . . Professionally, I've enrolled back in college and continue to pursue my degree. I update my resume

research spotlight

In a study of 495 women in engineering and science, researchers Kathleen Buse and Diana Bilimoria at Case Western Reserve University found that women who persisted in these careers often have a personal vision. The personal vision included their profession but wasn't limited to it. Having a vision enabled them to overcome the bias, barriers, and discrimination they encountered in their workplaces. The findings validated previous studies that self-efficacy, hope, and optimism are important elements of an individual's personal vision and core identity and necessary for that vision to be effective. Having clarity around the ideal self positively affected the women's work engagement, and work engagement directly affected the women's commitment to remain in an engineering field.

Source: K. Buse and D. Bilimoria, "Personal Vision: Enhancing Work Engagement and the Retention of Women in the Engineering Profession," *Frontiers in Psychology* 5, article 1400 (2014), doi.org/10.3389/fpsyg.2014.01400.

and apply for positions that I want and not just what I'm qualified for. I was recently promoted and I'm currently interviewing for the next level of management role. After completing my vision, I realized that my company values are directly in line with my personal values, which makes my decision to stay and pursue positions within the organization so easy.

crafting a vision

Creating a vision can be best considered as a process of crafting that requires us to be imaginative and creative. The best way to help someone identify their ideal self and convey their personal vision is to encourage them to *dream*. A favorite exercise in our leadership development programs is called "Catch Your Dreams" (more pragmatic folks call it the "Bucket List" exercise). The activity asks individuals to consider twenty-seven things that they would like to experience, try, or accomplish in their lifetime. After attempting to write as many as possible on a number of sticky notes, the person is asked to place the notes on a flip chart, then group those ideas into themes. Some examples are: career, family, travel, health, adventure, etc. In group settings, a good next step is to allow time for a "gallery walk." This is when people can walk around reading others' flip charts and viewing them as if they are fine art.

Most people enjoy the experience and find it helpful in imagining possibilities. We often see smiles, hear the laughter, and feel the positive energy in the group. Doing this exercise with a work group or even your family is a great way for people to help each other dream. It's inspiring and humbling to get a glimpse into the dreams and aspirations of others around us—like peeking into another's soul. This is just one example of how to prime and facilitate an experience of dreaming and discovery. See the reflection and application exercises at the end of the chapter for additional suggestions.

For many people, coaching and developing a vision for their future is mainly about work and their career. But the stories of courageous and curious people we have told so far show that work is but one part of our lives. While our professional lives can be a source of enjoyment and satisfaction, it's often the activities outside of work that fulfill a deeper sense of purpose and meaning. Amy Szabo found that things she was doing with other hospital executives that were not part of her day job were actually the activities that left her feeling the most satisfied and energized. Helping others was bigger and more meaningful than leading a hospital department. It tapped into Amy's sense of purpose. In our work as coaches, we've found that helping people uncover a *holistic* view of their hopes and dreams—one that considers and integrates all aspects of life—helps them to connect with and to develop a more comprehensive and authentic image of who they are, including passion, purpose, values, and identity. The process of helping a person discover her personal vision begins by asking her to reflect on her future life and work: her dreams and hopes regarding her physical health, romantic life and friendships, family health, spiritual health, community involvement, financial matters, and more. Of course, considering one's work (whether paid or not) is a part of the reflective process, but we do not presume that it's the center of a person's dream. Often, as we've seen in several examples in this book, coaching conversations equally encompass our professional *and* personal identities and activities.

All helping and coaching is about change or how to maintain a desired change that has occurred. For change to be ignited and sustained, a personal vision provides the essential foundation because it is a meaningful expression of a person's passion, purpose, and values. It is a comprehensive image of what we wish to do and who we wish to be in our lives. Crafting a personal vision is an iterative process that is different for each individual. But regardless of how the process unfolds, it will be obvious to the coach when the vision is "well-baked" because the individual is often filled with energy and can't wait to get started. This is inspiration and intrinsic motivation in action.

In chapter 7, we'll focus on what the coach, manager, or other helper can do to nurture a high-quality relationship with the individuals they help, in order to sustain that energy and help them turn dreams into reality.

key learning points

1. A personal vision is a holistic, comprehensive expression of a person's ideal self and ideal future, including dreams, sense of calling, passion, purpose, and core values.

2. A personal vision should be more like a visual dream than specific goals.

3. A personal vision should be highly important and meaningful to the person.

4. Although some aspects of a person's personal vision will change during various phases of life and work, others, such as core values and a sense of purpose, often remain the same.

reflection and application exercises

EXERCISE A: CATCH YOUR DREAMS

You will need a pack of sticky notes and a large piece of flip chart paper for this exercise. Using the notes, list things you would like to do or experience in your lifetime until you get to twenty-seven. Write each idea on a separate note. These are things that you've not yet begun or completed. Some tips to help: allow yourself to think freely and without imposing practical constraints. Reflect back to your childhood and what you dreamed of doing someday. Turn off the inner critic—it's impossible to dream while simultaneously being judged.

After your best attempt to write as many as possible, place your notes on a piece of flip-chart paper and group them into themes; for example: career, family, travel, health, adventure, spirituality, material goods, professional development, recreation. Write the theme near the sticky note groupings.

This exercise can be easily adapted to groups. Individuals would follow the steps above. Once every person has a flip chart with sticky notes grouped into themes, ask everyone to post their flip charts on a wall in the room. Then, allow time for a "gallery walk." A gallery walk provides an opportunity for everyone to walk around the room and view others' dreams. Be sure to add the guideline to approach viewing as if looking at fine art—with humble curiosity, appreciation, and even admiration. Individuals sometimes like to add a brief, personal note of inspiration to others' flip charts. Some examples of what we've observed are: "You inspire me," "You got this," "Very cool," and so forth. The key is for comments to be respectful and affirmative in nature and not evaluative or laden with advice.

EXERCISE B: MY VALUES

You'll find a list of values, beliefs, or personal characteristics for your consideration below. Identify which are most important to you and are guiding principles in your life. It is difficult to choose, of course, because many of these values and characteristics will be at least somewhat important to you. It is also hard to choose because you might find yourself thinking, "I *should* value X and put it first on my list," even though it really isn't. So force yourself to choose, and choose based upon your true feelings, not the *shoulds* in life.

You might find it useful to determine the degree of importance by imagining how you would feel if you were forced to give up believing in or acting on a particular value, belief, or personal characteristic. Or, think about how you would feel if your life revolved around certain values and beliefs. How would this make you feel? Sometimes you might find it helpful to consider two values at a time, asking yourself about the relative importance of one over the other.

1. Start by circling the fifteen or so values that are most important to you.

2. Then from this list, identify the ten that are most important to you and write them in a list.

3. From this list of ten, circle the top five that are most important to you and then rank them from most important to least important.

Values, Beliefs, or Desirable Personal Characteristics

Accomplishment	Ambitious	Belonging
Achievement	Assisting others	Broad-minded
Adventure		Caring
Affection	Authority	Challenge
Affectionate	Autonomy	Cheerful
Affiliation	Beauty	Clean

Comfortable life

Companionship

Compassion

Competent

Competitiveness

Conformity

Contentedness

Contribution to others

Control

Cooperation

Courageous

Courteous

Creativity

Dependable

Disciplined

Economic security

Effective

Equality

Excitement

Fame

Family happiness

Family security

Forgiving

Free choice

Freedom

Friendship

Fun

Genuineness

Happiness

Health

Helpfulness

Honesty

Hope

Imagination

Improving society

Independence

Innovative

Integrity

Intellectual

Involvement

Joy

Leisurely

Logical

Love

Loving

Mature love

National security

Nature

Obedient

Order

Peace

Personal development

Pleasure

Polite

Power

Pride

Rational

Recognition

Reliable

Religion

Respectful

Responsible

Restrained

Salvation

Self-controlled

Self-reliance

Self-respect

Sincerity

Spirituality	Taking risks	Tranquility
Stability	Teamwork	Wealth
Status	Tender	Winning
Success	Tidy	Wisdom
Symbolic		

My Ten Most Important Values

1. _____

2. _____

3. _____

4. _____

5. _____

6. _____

7. _____

8. _____

9. _____

10. _____

My Five Most Important Values

Finally, rank each of your five most important values, beliefs, or characteristics, with "1" being the most important value to you, to "5" being the least important of these five values.

1. _____

2. _____

3. _____

4. _____

5. _____

EXERCISE C: WINNING THE LOTTERY

You've just won the super lottery and received $80 million. How would your life and work change?

EXERCISE D: A DAY IN YOUR LIFE . . . FIFTEEN YEARS FROM NOW

It is fifteen years from today. You are living your ideal life. You are living in a location that you have always dreamed about. You are living with the people with whom you most want to be living. If work is part of your ideal image, you are doing the type and amount of work you love.

A netcam is attached to your shirt or blouse. What images would we see in a video stream of your day? Where would you be? What are you doing? Who else is there?

EXERCISE E: MY LEGACY

What would you wish to have as your legacy in life? In other words, what will remain or continue as a result of you having lived and worked all of these years?

Source: These exercises are reproduced from Richard Boyatzis, *The Ideal Self Workbook* (1999), used at Case Western Reserve University in courses and programs, and were printed in A. McKee, R. E. Boyatzis, and F. Johnston, *Becoming a Resonant Leader* (Boston: Harvard Business School Press, 2008); and R. Boyatzis and A. McKee, *Resonant Leadership: Renewing Yourself and Connecting with Others through Mindfulness, Hope, and Compassion* (Boston: Harvard Business School Press, 2005); and used in the Coursera massive open online course, *Inspiring Leadership through Emotional Intelligence.*

conversation guide

1. Share any three core values that are at the top of your list. Pick one, define what it means to you in your own words, and think of an example of how the value plays out in your life. Take turns each sharing your value, definition, and example. When listening to others, take care to not evaluate or critique their values.

2. As we suggested in chapter 3, think about the social and professional/organizational relationships in your life. Of the people who you spend the most time with or those with whom you are

the closest, who among them really "gets" you or understands what really "makes you tick"?

3. What are your social identity groups? For example, what do you wear with pride? What fan sports clubs do you belong to? Are you part of some neighborhood or religious community from which you draw pride and a sense of belonging? In what ways do your current social identity groups help you move closer to your ideal self and personal vision?

cultivating a resonant relationship

listen beyond what you hear

Sean Hannigan (not his real name) was a well-regarded, success-ful executive at a US-based, multinational industrial organization. With twenty-five years of experience under his belt, he was a mas-ter at overseeing the technical complexities of the finance functions he led and was rewarded with promotion upon promotion, leading to his role of chief financial officer.

Given his professional success, Sean was surprised at some neg-ative feedback he received from a 360-degree assessment of his emotional and social intelligence competencies, completed by his bosses, peers, and subordinates.[1] The assessment was part of a leadership development program in which he was paired with an executive coach. The coach had already helped Sean to develop his personal vision. Now it was time to review the 360 feedback.

"What's your reaction to this feedback?" she asked him.

Sean flipped through the pages rapidly and stopped halfway through. He looked at his coach and said, "The feedback was good overall. I was pleasantly surprised by the strengths that others noticed. I've heard some of this feedback before, but it's easy to lose sight of what you do well when you're in the trenches working through problems, as I tend to do all the time." She nudged him further to describe his most distinctive strengths, based on the assessment, and how those were visible to others.

After a lengthy discussion about his positive feedback, Sean's coach asked, "What else?"

Sean looked down at the assessment and said, "It's pretty clear that my peers and direct reports don't feel that I listen to them well, or sometimes at all. It's a definite theme."

His coach probed, "Do you think it's valid?" Sean thought for a moment. "Well, it's hard to deny it when several people commented on it. When I step back and think about it, I can see their point. My schedule is pretty full and I don't have time to waste on small talk." Sean and his coach spent more time working through other feedback in the report until they had distilled it down into a personal balance sheet of his assets and liabilities (i.e., strengths and weaknesses).

Then she asked, "What do you feel drawn to work on? Where can you give the greatest amount of energy?" Without missing a beat, Sean responded. "Definitely becoming a better listener. Out of all this feedback, it bothers me the most. But I'm not sure how to improve that exactly."

Fortunately, Sean's coach knew how to help him with the changes he wished to make. She had already begun a fundamental step in the process: building a positive coaching relationship. Although Sean had a lot of experience working with others both inside and outside the company, building effective working relationships with his managers or peers, let alone his direct reports, had never been a priority. He tended to view work relationships as the means to achieving a task or as resources needed to complete a project.

Unlike other advisers, like his accountant, lawyer, or physician, Sean's coach sought to create a trusting, supportive, resonant relationship, the kind we first discussed in chapters 2 and 3. She first built rapport with him by inquiring about his professional and personal journey and being interested to know his story. She also asked about his desired outcomes for their coaching engagement, summarizing those in a document to anchor their process. In subsequent sessions, she prioritized his goals and agenda for their time together and regularly asked what he was taking away from their conversations to help him reflect. And while she asked a number of questions designed to help Sean connect with the best of who he was as a person and a leader, she spent the majority of time actively listening and serving as a mirror back to him of what she heard.

This process enabled Sean's coach not just to know him but to connect with him on a deeper level. It also helped to create a psychologically safe space where he could think and reflect without the threat of being judged. It's unlikely that Sean would have been as open and committed to improve his own deficiencies if he'd been reluctant to examine the data honestly with this coach, or if he'd felt threatened or defensive in her presence. Ultimately, what Sean's coach did was to demonstrate that she cared about him as a person and wanted him to succeed, which in turn allowed trust to take root and blossom in their coaching relationship.

The relationship between a helper of any kind and the individual being helped is the heart of any change process. We will return to Sean's story later in this chapter as we explore the coaching relationship and some cornerstones for how to build and nurture an effective one. We'll also look at how the helper's own internal preparation affects the interaction, and how active listening is key. But first, let's explore how to develop a resonant relationship with those we strive to coach and help.

what makes a resonant relationship?

Inspiring, meaningful coaching moments and high-quality, trusting coaching relationships don't just happen. They take intention, preparation, and practice. At its very core, a high-quality relationship between, say, a manager and an employee is shaped by the ongoing interactions and conversations between the two individuals. When you are trying or hoping to help people, your primary role as helper is to facilitate self-directed learning and development for the other person. Effective developmental conversations are shaped by the quality of the discrete connections we form, our ability to listen deeply and remain fully present, as well as the encouragement we extend to inspire the other person to learn, grow, and change through meaningful discussions.

Our Weatherhead colleague John Paul Stephens expanded on work originally done by Jane Dutton and Emily Heaphy to describe a high-quality connection (HQC)—a connection that is a positive, dyadic, short-term interaction. Experiencing an HQC leaves you feeling alive, uplifted, energetic, and genuinely cared for.[2] Positive regard in the interaction goes both ways, meaning it is mutual. Both parties exchange feelings of compassion rooted in an experience of shared vulnerability and responsiveness to each other. Stephens, Heaphy, and Dutton propose that underlying cognitive, emotional and behavioral mechanisms might explain high-quality connections.

High-quality connections breathe life into both the helper and the individual being helped whenever they meet—and provide the foundation for a longer-term, resonant relationship to grow, just as shared vision, compassion, and energy arouse the PEA and its renewing effects on each person. Positive, life-giving connections are essential to establish trust and convey and experience support. As Dutton and Heaphy explain, even short-term exchanges between people can result in a high-quality connection, which they describe through three structural dimensions: *emotional carrying capacity*, *tensility*, and the *degree of connectivity*.[3] Emotional carrying capacity allows a full range of positive and negative emotions to be shared. Tensility refers to the capacity of the connection to adapt and bounce back through various situations and contexts. The degree of connectivity describes the extent to which the connection encourages generativity and openness to new ideas. Dimensions such as emotional carrying capacity have been associated with higher resilience in individuals and their teams. Essentially, sharing more emotions in relationships helps people to be more resilient.[4]

Scholars Kathy Kram and Wendy Murphy suggest that for helping relationships to have transformational impact, the connection needs to be positive and mutually shared. Both the coach or helper and the person being helped have positive mutual regard for each other, share a commitment to their relationship, and benefit equally from their engagement and interactions. Such relationships help foster openness to learning and change. This often sets coaching, mentoring, or even a relationship with a manager apart as a developmental relationship from typical work relationships or even traditional mentoring, where the mentor merely advises the mentee. At its core, such a relationship is a developmental partnership where the primary focus of the experience is to stimulate and support learning. This could be personal, professional, or task-related learning, or some combination of those.[5]

We know from research that individuals are affected by interactions with others through the power of emotional contagion and social mimicry. That's why the *quality* of a coaching, managing, or helping relationship is an important consideration. For individuals and teams seeking to change, the relationships form the foundation of support, challenge, learning, and encouragement between individuals.[6] In our roles as coaches and helpers, it's important to remember that we have a profound impact on each other's moods and emotional states, so we need to be mindful of whom we are infecting with our moods and emotions.[7]

In the model of Intentional Change Theory presented in chapter 3, resonant relationships are at the center and affect each of the phases of sustained, desired change and the transitions from one phase to another. Keep in mind that development and change is a nonlinear and uneven process—it evolves for many people as a series of fits and starts. Personal self-awareness doesn't happen automatically or in a vacuum; otherwise, we would all be highly attuned to our feelings and the reasons behind them. Pressure at work and family demands often work against our best intentions to increase self-awareness and growth. When we are able to sustain the efforts of a growth process, it's usually because we have support from one, two, or a network of people. As discussed in earlier chapters, we call these *resonant relationships* because they embody support, security, and safety and infuse us with the energy and motivation to reflect authentically, take initiative, and keep trying.

Let's return to Sean's story. One thing his coach did to nurture a resonant relationship was to demonstrate sincere interest in getting to know him. She also expressed a genuine desire to help him. She created an environment where he could reflect openly and honestly without fear of being judged. This provided Sean with a sense of trust and psychological safety. She nudged him to name his core values and strengths aloud and articulate the unique meaning he ascribed to them. As we will examine further in this chapter, those are the type of discussions that foster a shared vision and unleash shared positive energy, connecting the coach, manager, or other helper to the person being helped. Sean could see that his coach appreciated and recognized his positive qualities, giving him a sense of feeling understood and seen as a whole person, with strengths as well as weaknesses and a capacity to elevate his capability and reach success. This element of their relationship was significant in motivating him to take a step forward. If he couldn't view his capabilities in a holistic way, considering distinctive strengths equally with struggles, he would likely feel either too defensive or too discouraged to work on what he wanted to change, such as improving his listening skills.

In their next session, the coach wanted to get a sense of Sean's typical day before working with him on a plan to help him become a better listener. She had already learned that his job entailed supporting the CEO in strategically leading the global enterprise by overseeing financial operations across the globe and with his C-suite peers. He had a good rapport with Wall Street analysts and enjoyed preparing for quarterly investor calls. Sean's team of direct reports included eight heads of finance for the enterprise and the various business units around the world.

"Let's say I'm one of your direct reports," the coach began. "Walk me through a typical day and how we interact. Let's start with the physical space. Tell me about your office. What do I see?"

Sean proceeded, "I have a desk facing the window with two computers on it, one for internal company business and another to follow stock activity. There's another desk in front facing the door and my chair sits in between. When I'm in the office, I spend most of my time looking at these screens."

"So, with your back to the door?" the coach inquired.

"Pretty much."

"Ok," she said. "So let's say that I come to talk with you, either planned or unplanned. What happens then?" Sean described scenarios where a direct report or peer would stand in the doorway while he remained glued to the two screens, with his back to them. He explained that he detested "meetings for the sake of meetings," so he kept conversations short and sweet. He also didn't like to micromanage, so unless there was an important update or a problem that someone needed help in solving, he didn't see much need to meet, and he kept those discussions to ten or fifteen minutes, often while the person remained standing.

In the 360 feedback, Sean's staff and peers reported feeling as if he didn't have time for them and didn't care to listen to what they had to say. Now, in the conversation with his coach, it was dawning on Sean that the quality of the relationship he had with others was functional and purely focused on a task or problem solving. Confronted with that realization, he looked at his coach and said, "No wonder people don't feel like I listen to them! They must think I'm a jerk!" His coach didn't agree with his entire self-assessment, but she did agree with one thing. Most of the time, he paid more attention to the problem or task and not the person—and this was an obstacle for his ability to lead the team effectively.

Over the following months, Sean experimented with new behaviors to adjust the ways in which he interacted with his direct reports and peers. His goal was to build a better working relationship with others. This included getting out from behind his desk and away from the flashing computer screens, which were a major distraction. Sean began by meeting with people in a conference room and later at a small table in his office. He scheduled monthly meetings with his direct reports, with no agenda. They could use the time in whatever way they wanted. His job was to ask a few questions and mostly listen. He was intentional about finding a place to meet with minimal distractions. It felt strange at first, and he battled thoughts that it was a colossal waste of time. But then, in a matter of months, Sean noticed that people were more open with him and shared more information. He knew more about the people around him in terms of what they had going on at work and even outside of work, and he felt more connected to them.

Sean's story illustrates how sometimes the smallest steps—in this case, getting out from behind his desk, being genuinely interested in engaging with people, and actively listening to people—can lead to the biggest outcomes. That's because behavior change is fundamentally about changing our thoughts and habits one step at a time.

But Sean's story is also about a resonant coaching relationship and what a coach can do to develop one. Along with colleagues from the Coaching Research Lab at Case Western Reserve University, we have collectively studied *quality* within relationships in various contexts over the past twelve years. We define a quality relationship along three dimensions: the degree of shared vision, shared compassion, and shared relational energy—much like what we described in the coaching relationship with Sean. We've seen how those three elements repeatedly have a strong, positive impact on a host of leadership and organizational outcomes such as engagement, effectiveness, and well-being.[8]

In the same way as an individual embarking on change is aided by a personal vision to sustain the change she hopes to make, a shared vision between a coach and coachee helps to create a bigger, hope-filled image of the future. A sense of purpose replaces goals and tasks as the reason for their interactions. Whether the relationship is between a manager and subordinate, teacher and student, doctor and patient, or spouses, having a shared sense of purpose feels bigger than a task of managing time better, trying to exercise more, or planning a family vacation. When two or more people create a shared vision, they resonate by connecting deeply. Their conversations feel more meaningful beyond just accomplishing short-term goals. They seem to move in sync with one another.

research spotlight

Faculty and doctoral students in the Department of Organizational Behavior and the Coaching Research Lab at the Weatherhead School of Management conducted a wide range of studies examining the influence of shared vision, shared compassion, and relational energy on the ability to create a positive or negative emotion in a variety of applications. PEA and NEA in relationships were measured first by the PNEA (positive-negative emotional attractors) Survey and later updated to its current form—the Relational Climate Survey.[9] We provide a high-level summary of many studies below.

- Three hundred and seventy-five Type II diabetic patients working with doctors who created a shared vision around their desired future health followed the doctor's instructions—what is called *treatment adherence*—more than doctor-patient relationships characterized differently.[10]

- Eighty-five senior banking leaders worked with a coach in two sessions; relationship quality was measured through two instruments—the PNEA and the Perceived Quality of the Employee Coaching Relationship (PQECR)—and found that a quality coaching relationship amplified the impact of emotional and social intelligence competencies on the leaders' personal vision, work engagement, and career satisfaction.[11]

- Shared compassion among IT managers and professions predicted engagement on two different scales.[12]

- In a study of 218 community college presidents, shared vision led to increased engagement on the part of faculty.[13]

- Physicians who were more effective leaders had doctor-patient relationships characterized by shared vision and that amplified the impact of their social intelligence competencies.[14]

- When executives in high-tech firms had working relationships with their direct reports characterized by greater shared vision, compassion, and relational energy, their units produced more product innovations than others.[15]

- When the relationships in a family business experienced more shared vision, financial performance over the following five years and development of the next generation of leaders was significantly better.[16]

- Daughters who had a shared vision with their fathers were more likely to become the successors and CEOs of family businesses than their brothers.[17]

- The effect on team-member engagement from the collective emotional competencies of team members in consulting and manufacturing was amplified by the degree of shared vision they perceived in their teams.[18]

- Engineers felt dramatically more engaged in their project in the R&D division of a major international manufacturing firm when they perceived a greater degree of shared vision within the team.[19]

The foundation for a true partnership emerges from a shared commitment—at both rational and emotional levels—to each other and what's possible, not just to an exchange of ideas. While shared vision spreads the feeling of hope and purpose, shared compassion spreads the feeling of caring. It involves the kind of mutual caring and trust that leaves both parties feeling appreciated and cared for. Mutual or shared compassion (i.e., caring for each other as people, not just their roles) is the glue that keeps helpers and the

the ethics of coaching

If you work as a professional coach, you must follow important codes of behavior. These codes of behavior ensure that the profession of coaching upholds the highest standards of professionalism. Adhering to ethical guidelines is often required for membership in various coaching networks, so be sure to become familiar with existing codes of ethics. Although we're unable to include every coaching organization's codes, there are two in particular with well-developed, publicly available codes of ethics: the Center for Credentialing and Education (CCE) and the International Coach Federation (ICF). The codes of behavior suggested by both organizations cover topics such as professional conduct with clients, conflict of interest, and matters of confidentiality and privacy. Their websites provide additional information.

But we would also say that, given the interpersonal nature of helping others, ethical considerations are important for everyone to keep in mind. In general, four universal principles serve as an important foundation for any coaching endeavor—be it as a manager, teacher, parent, doctor, cleric, and so forth. First, remember that flourishing is the main goal. Above all else, our primary aim in coaching is to help others realize their aspirations and grow into the best version of themselves. Borrowing language from Barbara Frederickson, the spirit of the coach's work is *to broaden and build*—it is never to manipulate or control. Second—and this one obviously applies mainly to professional coaches—always have a contract, whether your work is sponsored by an individual or an organization. It should be a written contract that is agreed on and signed by all parties involved, specifying roles, responsibilities, and expectations. It's also useful to include elements of the coaching process and the time period for the work to be completed.

Third, maintain confidentiality. The relationship between a coach and coachee can be deep and complex. In all cases, it requires confidentiality. As a coach, manager, or other helper, you must maintain the individual's right to privacy. Keeping your conversation just between the two of you also signals you are trustworthy. Trust is fragile. It can take years to build it and a minute of poor judgment to lose it. (If you're a professional coach, include language on upholding confidentiality in your contract. Discuss it at the beginning of your coaching engagement, specifying how and through what means you'll exchange information.)

Fourth, know your boundaries and keep them clear between you and the individual you're helping. If the individual discloses or you become aware of extenuating personal or even medical issues that extend beyond the scope of your coaching abilities, make a referral to another professional who can help that person. Examples of issues you might encounter are personal family matters such as a divorce or maybe a troubled child, mental health concerns such as depression or anxiety, financial struggles and concerns, or issues of illegal activity. Equally important when it comes to boundaries is maintaining a professional relationship (unless, of course, it's your child or a friend you are coaching!). This can sometimes be hard to tease out because, when done well, the coaching relationship results in both parties feeling connected and close. Stay mindful, therefore, of the well-being of the person you are helping by remembering not to allow the lines between a professional and personal or romantic relationship to become blurred.

These are general guidelines and we share them only as a starting point. They aren't meant to be a comprehensive list in any way. The best guideline is to mindfully uphold the intention in coaching to "do no harm." And if you are a professional coach, always stay abreast of current ethical guidelines and be attuned to potential ethical concerns.

people they help closely connected to one another. By facilitating hope, optimism, mindfulness, caring, and playfulness in the relationship, individuals activate the PEA in themselves as well as those they seek to inspire and help, unleashing health benefits and other advantages, as discussed in chapter 3.

Beyond shared vision and shared compassion, other researchers offer additional considerations around what elements of coaching relationships are notable and relevant. Scholars at the University of Akron suggest that high-quality coaching relationships are characterized by four dimensions: genuineness of the relationship; effective communication; comfort with the relationship; and the extent to which the collaboration facilitates development.[20] Another team of researchers studied coaching relationships in a military service academy and found rapport, trust, and commitment to be important.[21] (For key caveats to keep in mind when developing a coaching relationship, see the sidebar "The Ethics of Coaching.")

the coaching mindset

As a coach, your frame of mind is as important as the skills you bring to the coaching conversation. When you're feeling internally off-balance, you are unlikely to make much progress in a coaching situation. Preparation and readiness are everything, as is practice. Throughout this book we've discussed how coaching comes in many different forms—and one key way that many of us have "coached" others is as parents, particularly around transitions in our children's lives. Consider the following story from Ellen, one of this book's authors, about her efforts to coach her daughter around making choices about her future.

One fall evening in Maureen's senior year of high school, Ellen arrived home late from a full day of teaching to find her husband putting dinner on the table. What a relief! It had been a long day and she remembered that the refrigerator was empty since she hadn't made it to the grocery store, so this was a welcome gift. She'd also fought rush-hour traffic and highway construction to attend an information meeting at Maureen's school about applying for and paying for college.

Throughout the meeting, as the school counselors presented a barrage of details, Ellen felt her stress level rising. "When did the college application process become so complex?" she wondered. She also found herself daydreaming about how simple life had seemed when Maureen was a child. "Wasn't it just yesterday that I attended the parent meeting for kindergarten?" Where did the time go?" The counselors reviewed important steps that the students needed to follow—everything from registering for the last round of standardized tests to finalizing the list of schools to apply to and writing application essays. Ellen left the meeting with three pages of notes and a headache.

Hungry and whipped from the day, she sat down at the dinner table with family. Ellen was anxious to talk with Maureen and share what she'd learned at the parent meeting. She asked her with genuine curiosity, "Do you have new thoughts about the schools you want to apply to?"

"Yeah, I think so," Maureen responded flatly. "But I'd like to check out a few more schools." This was a surprise to Ellen. They'd already spent the summer visiting several colleges, and Maureen had compiled a list of five to seven colleges she was interested in. Sitting at the kitchen table, Ellen could feel her own anxiety, which had begun at the parent meeting, rising. Still, she reminded herself that her daughter probably was feeling overwhelmed by the choices she needed to make.

Ellen decided to pursue another line of questioning. As gently as she could, she asked, "How are your essays coming along?" College admission counselors all offered the same advice: as soon as the applications open, start drafting your essays—and don't wait until the last minute. For reasons that Ellen couldn't figure out, Maureen, who was a strong student, had procrastinated all summer and seemed reluctant to get started on her essays. It was like she was paralyzed to engage in the process.

"I haven't started them yet," Maureen responded, looking annoyed. "We're going to work on them in English class next week."

Suddenly, it was as though a switch went off in Ellen. The full impact of her own feelings of being overwhelmed and fatigued suddenly took over, and she responded angrily, "What in the world is the problem? You've had all summer. It's time to stop stalling and start writing!"

Then, silence. Maureen glared out the window. Immediately, Ellen regretted what she said and felt remorseful. Clearly that interaction hadn't gone so well. She wanted to be helpful but had failed. She knew that she'd just lost one chance, at least, of making a positive connection with her daughter and actually encouraging her to start on her essays. By allowing herself to get frustrated by Maureen's response, she stopped listening and being empathetic.

Later, Ellen reflected on what she could have done differently. Most importantly, she would have taken stock of her emotional and physical state *before* attempting to enter into such a potentially charged conversation. Had she been more self-aware, she would have realized she was tired and not in a good place to coach or even fully listen. Then, perhaps on another day when both she and Maureen were more relaxed, she could try again. This time, she'd remember her own teenage years and try to be more empathetic to the pressure on her daughter to figure out her life. She would try to walk alongside her, so to speak, rather than sit across from Maureen and ask more questions anchored in the positive emotional attractor. For example, questions such as "What are you excited to learn, try, and accomplish at college?" or "What subjects in school do you enjoy so much that you can't wait for the next class?" That might help open up Maureen to her possibilities and personal vision—as opposed to firing guilt-inducing questions at her, which had only triggered stress and anxiety and shut her down more.

As Ellen's parenting story illustrates all too clearly, the frame of mind and emotional state of anyone who tries to help another is fundamental to how the conversation will unfold. Next we share some basic guidelines for ensuring more mindful coaching interactions.

cornerstones of coaching

We offer three cornerstones to help you approach coaching interactions with a mindset for building and nurturing a quality coaching relationship. First, *believe that individual change is a process, not an event*. Growth and development take time. In pursuit of new habits, it takes practice and feedback to grow one's openness, awareness, and energy to think and behave differently. This is just as true for the helper as it is for the person seeking to change or on the receiving end of help. We all need to allow ourselves room to make mistakes and to grow and improve. The process doesn't happen overnight, although we often forget this under time pressures and daily stress.

For example, Ellen's efforts to coach her daughter about her future didn't begin just that evening at the dinner table. Ellen had been helping Maureen for the past year to consider careers and colleges that could be a good fit for her. So the process of trying to help Maureen to discern what she wanted to do and explore the right college for her was unfolding over time. But in that particular moment at dinner, Ellen slipped into negativity and expected immediate answers, which never works when we're trying to genuinely help. Fortunately, she and her daughter already had a lifetime of building a bond, and Ellen knew she would be able to work with her daughter once she had replenished her own inner resources and equilibrium.

Second, *consider your approach to coaching as a chance to mine for gold, not dig for dirt*. A story appeared in the *Houston Business Journal* years ago that's become a favorite in our coach education and certification programs.[22] In the late nineteenth century, Andrew Carnegie was one of the wealthiest individuals in America. A poor immigrant from Scotland, he worked many jobs as a young man, eventually becoming the leader of the largest steel manufacturer in the country. At one point, Carnegie had many millionaires working for him, which was quite rare for the times. A reporter curious to understand his secrets interviewed Carnegie, inquiring how it was possible to have paid that much money to so many people. Carnegie shared that people are developed the same way that gold is mined. "Several tons of dirt must be moved to get an ounce of gold, but you don't go into the mine looking for dirt. You go into the mine looking for gold." Excellent coaches approach coaching conversations looking for the gold in the other person or group. This is common sense but uncommon practice—and even with the best of intentions, the best coaches can miss this golden opportunity. As in Ellen's story with her daughter, by getting emotionally charged, she missed an important opportunity to help Maureen connect with her strengths and see her own unique gifts and instead shut down any dialogue, at least temporarily.

Third, consider that *the agenda for the conversation should come from the person being coached.* This means that, although the coach is the keeper of the overall process, the fundamental reason for the process is to help the other person—not for the coach to share his advice or experience. So, keep the agenda flexible and meet others wherever they are. As keepers of the process, it's important to know the end goal and stay true to it but allow the individual to have a say and choice in how you use your time together more often than not. As illustrated in Ellen's story, one pitfall was that she drove the agenda for the conversation with her daughter rather than inviting Maureen to talk, and because she'd failed to check her own energy, she was unable to respond as empathetically as she would have liked.

Apart from those three basic guidelines, the most important ingredient for establishing a high-quality coaching relationship is being fully present and being mindful of yourself as well as the other person. Even the most experienced coaches have to work at it every time they coach. One crucial element for nurturing trust and demonstrating support is to pay close attention, deeply and actively listening to the other person. We'll explore this further in the next section.

listen beyond what you hear

Recall Sean's story and how, after a lengthy discussion about his positive feedback, Sean's coach asked a crucial question: "What else?"

Sean was able then to admit to the negative feedback he'd also read and how it was bugging him. "What else?" (also "Tell me more") is one of our favorite questions, one that we always encourage our students to include in their coaching conversations. The question itself has an inviting effect because it communicates an interest in other people's thoughts-beneath-their-thoughts. It also conveys an openness to hear whatever it is that the individual might be reluctant to say. Often the question elicits revelations that might surprise even the responder.

Recall for a moment a time when you held someone else's attention, when you knew the person was completely focused on what you were saying and intent on understanding your idea or feeling. If you are like most people, it felt great! You felt respected, cared for, even loved. You felt special. At a basic human level, we all want to be understood and appreciated and when we take the time to listen to another person, we demonstrate that we care and value what they have to say.

Listening is key to helping us resonate with others around us. It allows people to trust and feel trusted in return. By feeling safe psychologically and emotionally, listening encourages the other person to feel safe psychologically and emotionally, and therefore be open to new ideas and experiences. But in the workplace, the importance of deep listening is often trumped by the pressure to perform and demonstrate expertise.

To listen is to hear with thoughtful attention.[23] Active listening is giving your full attention to the other person and listening with all of your senses. Your intention in active listening is to fully understand the other person's idea or message and demonstrate respect for their point of view, even if you disagree with it. Through your words and nonverbal cues, you should strive to convey that you may or may not agree with the other person, but first that you want to understand their thoughts and feelings and that you accept and respect what they have to say.

Most of us struggle when it comes to listening. We interrupt people. We finish the other person's sentences. We evaluate what they are saying. Within thirty seconds, the judge within us not only decides that we know what the other person is thinking, feeling, and about to say, but often, we can't resist the urge to tell him in the form of a suggestion, advice, or a command.

In a pivotal article published in 1952 in *Harvard Business Review*, Carl Rogers and F. J. Roethlisberger, professors at Harvard Business School, suggested that the urge to quickly evaluate what we hear is automatic and instinctive. It creates a barrier to listening, open communication, and learning. When we hear a statement made by someone, we immediately have a tendency to agree or disagree and have a reaction not just to what the person said, but also to our own thoughts in response. When deep feelings arise within the conversation, our reaction takes on a degree of emotional intensity. Dialogue shuts down as tempers and tensions rise, stalling any hope of learning or understanding.[24]

In coaching, further breakdowns in listening can occur—paradoxically because of the fundamental job of the coach, which is to exercise self-awareness and emotional self-control, especially when listening. But this can be a double-edged sword. Such self-control isn't easy and can actually activate the NEA *in the coach* as he actively resists the urge to speak!

It's true that the best coaches are great listeners. But as humans, we are all easily distracted. We get caught up in our own thoughts and while we think that we are actively listening to others, we often are anticipating what we have to say next. The extent of our ability and interest to listen is surface-level. We are listening to the conversation playing out inside our mind, not being fully present to listen to the other person.

Active listening takes a good deal of intention, effort, and energy. It starts with a deep and genuine self-awareness of who we are and what we bring to the coaching interaction. It includes being aware of our biases. In the words of gestalt psychotherapist Robert Lee, "Our assumptions and stereotypes create filters for how we hear people. We don't hear others from the place of who they are. We hear them through the filter of who we *think* they are. So, being aware of our implicit biases is essential to keep us honest and enable us to be open to listen fully to what the person in front of us, on the computer screen or on the phone has to say."[25]

research spotlight

Strengthening our awareness and skills to be attentive listeners has its benefits in solidifying coaching relationships that are positive and generative. Researchers Guy Itzchakov and Avi Kluger conducted several studies involving attentive and distracted listeners. In one study, 114 undergraduate students were randomly paired with attentive and distracted listeners. When speakers felt listened to by someone instructed to be attentive, they reported higher self-awareness, lower anxiety, and greater clarity around their attitudes than when they were matched with distracted listeners. They were able to reflect both strengths and weaknesses more than those paired with a distracted listener. They also reported more complex or multifaceted factors impacting their topic of discussion. They could think more holistically and envision to a greater degree. Drawing insights from their studies, the researchers advocate that attentive, empathic listening encourages others to feel relaxed, be more self-aware, and expand their capability to openly reflect.

Source: G. Itzchakov and A. Kluger, "The Power of Listening in Helping People Change," hbr.org, May 17, 2018.

Deep listening continues with being aware of the other person. Listening with all of our senses means that we hear, see, and feel what the other person shares, shows, and experiences. We hear words and are attentive to emotional and nonverbal cues. We dial in to language, facial expression, and tone. We see eyes light up, the furrowed brow, and the fidgeting in the chair. We hear changes in voice, pace of speech, and breath—all in service of seeking to understand and maintain a safe, supportive space for the person to reflect and learn.

In helping relationships, one internal resource that coaches and helpers rely on to be tuned into another individual is empathy. Empathy represents our ability to put ourselves in the shoes of another person (or group) and imagine what the individual is seeing, thinking, and feeling as if we were that individual while realizing that we are not. Our colleague Helen Riess, from the Harvard Medical School, suggests that we are hardwired to be empathetic through *mirror neurons*, which are specialized brain cells in the premotor cortex. She explains, "Before their discovery, scientists generally believed that our brains used logical thought processes to interpret and predict other people's actions. We now believe these neurological 'mirrors' and shared circuits give us the ability to *understand* not just what another is thinking but to *feel* what they are feeling as well." These specialized neurons allow us to connect cognitively with others, forming the basis of what Reiss calls *shared mind intelligence*—literally being in the same cognitive wavelength as another person.[26]

Empathy has three different facets—cognitive, emotional, and behavioral—that contribute to strengthening our bond or connection in our helping relationships.[27] *Cognitive empathy* involves conceptually understanding the perspective of another person and draws on the neural networks that involve analytical processing. It engages the analytical network as we focus our attention on collecting information to form a holistic picture of the person or situation and work to learn and absorb her perspective. *Emotional empathy* is the ability to be emotionally in tune with another person and feel what she feels. For example, this could be the excitement you feel when your coworker gets that promotion she's worked hard for or the sadness and heaviness you feel when your best friend's mother dies after an unexpected illness. Emotional empathy activates regions of our emotional brain center, or empathic network. We have an easier time accessing emotional empathy when we see ourselves as similar to another person (e.g., you grew up in the same hometown, played the same varsity sport in high school, share the same religious or political views). It's often not as immediate or instinctive when the differences between two people are great.

Behavioral empathy is the third facet of empathy. It is also known as *empathic concern*, as it is the motivation to respond to help another person in some way. It is when our thinking and feeling are integrated and propel us to want to do something. You demonstrate empathic concern when you feel that inner tug in your heart that requires you to act to help another person.

Depending on the unique disposition of the coach, an individual may respond differently to the range of emotional expressions that the coach might use. Being emotionally attuned creates an emotional connection, while an analytical approach may give the individual a sense that the coach is more interested in solving the perceived problem. There's no one best way. In reality, to truly help others, we need to utilize all forms of empathy: the ability to attune ourselves to others, the desire to understand others, and the willingness to be an active participant who helps others on their journey of development and change.

But for those of us who struggle to listen well, there is hope! Listening is an art and a skill that can be developed. Henry Kimsey-House and Karen Kimsey-House, along with colleagues Phillip Sandahl and Laura Whitworth, suggest that there are three levels of listening, through which connecting and coaching relationships take shape:[28]

- Level 1 listening, also known as the *connection level*, involves listening to others and deciding what their words mean to us personally. The listener emphasizes an inward focus; listening at this level is useful to establish common ground in conversations by connecting on a personal level with the other person.

- Level 2 listening is referred to as the *focused level*. This level involves giving full attention to the other person and demonstrating empathy and intuition to deeply understand and connect with those with whom we interact.

- Level 3 listening is the *global level* and involves listening with all of our senses and beyond just the words. While continuing to give full attention to the other person, we give a bigger context to what we hear and consider the broader environment and what is not being said in addition to what is being shared.

Listening at level 1 allows us to connect with other people. This is the listening that happens all the time in the workplace, when we meet someone at a networking event, or are in a team meeting together. One person talks about his weekend at his lake house. You just spent a weekend away renting a house on the same lake and you end up trading stories about favorite restaurants in the area. This is significant because connecting with others forms the basis for our professional and personal relationships. But to coach effectively, we need to go past just connecting to listen at levels 2 and 3. In order to establish a high-quality relationship and be truly helpful, we need to lean in and listen with all of our senses.

We offer two other simple tips to help you stay attentive and listen at your best. Remember the 80-20 rule. As a coach, manager, or other helper, aim to speak only 20 percent of the time, allowing the individual you're helping to speak 80 percent. This helps to reinforce that the focus is on the individual. Another favorite is the acronym WAIT, which stands for "Why am I talking?" If you find yourself taking up a lot of airspace, you're not coaching; you're either telling your own story or teaching or managing or directing. By remembering W-A-I-T, you can keep yourself on track. If you catch yourself talking too much, use a question to shift the focus away from you and your story and back to the person you are coaching.

We hope that you've found meaningful content and practical tips in this chapter to help you in your efforts to build and nurture high-quality helping relationships. In chapter 8, we'll explore how organizations strive to build a culture of coaching through a variety of approaches including peer coaching, managerial coaching, and using external coaches.

key learning points

1. The relationship between a coach and coachee or helper and person being helped is the heart of any developmental relation-

ship. The relationship needs to be *resonant* to be high quality, which means it is characterized by an overall positive emotional tone, a shared vision, and shared compassion.

2. When striving to coach or help others to change, approach the relationship with a coaching mindset. Change is a process, not an event, and it takes time. Believe that gold exists within every person and your main job is to help move tons of dirt to find the treasure. Stay focused on the other person, not on the process or the problem. Let the person drive the agenda more often than you do.

3. Deep, active listening on the part of the coach is fundamental and essential to build high-quality helping relationships.

reflection and application exercises

1. Over the course of the next week or so, notice the conversations you have with others. Note if and how other people listen to you, and how you listen to them. Note any patterns that emerge in these conversations with regard to how each person listens to each other.

2. During your ride to work (not recommended if you are the person driving) or some other moment of downtime early in your day, reflect on earlier interactions you had that morning with your spouse, partner, children, parents, or roommates. What did you talk about? How well did you listen? Did you hear what they were saying and how they felt about it?

3. Focus on one conversation at work each day, whether in a group meeting or a one-on-one conversation. Then talk to the person afterward and tell them what you heard and felt they were trying to communicate. Check to see if that is what they meant.

conversation guide

1. In your study group or among a group of colleagues, discuss observations that you had from a shared meeting. Did you observe people in the meeting who seemed to be actively listening and attentive to others? Did you observe people in the same meeting who seemed to be distracted or not attentive to others for whatever reason? What bearing did your observations have on the productivity of the meeting? How about on the relationships between people?

2. Thinking about the same meeting as the above activity, were there some people who seemed to be lecturing or talking *at* others rather than *with* them? What is it about these people's behavior or relationships with others that stands out? When you compare these individuals with those in the same meeting who were attentive and listening to others, what were the differences in how these two people were behaving?

3. Discuss the last time you were in a conversation (possibly with a spouse, partner, or coworker) when you felt the other person *seemed* to be paying attention but did not seem to be really listening. How did that make you feel?

creating a culture of coaching or helping

pathways to transform

the organization

When Jeff Darner, senior director of talent management and human resources, first brought coaching into Moen, a Fortune Brands company, he faced a grindingly slow process. As he said, the executives "were not used to asking people about how they feel."[1] What's more, Moen's managers already felt pressed for time to complete their daily work and saw developmental conversations as another task on their already lengthy lists. Little by little, through training and conversations, the climate changed. Managers who once felt they didn't have time to talk—much less listen—to each other, now take the time to do just that. They even report observable daily, informal coaching moments among managers and with staff members in the halls and after meetings.

That's the kind of coaching culture we are helping to create in the organizations in which we work, and now with this book we're trying to spread that learning. Specifically, an effective coaching culture develops in organizations where people have gained skills in helping other people through coaching to the positive emotional attractor.

In other settings—among our families or friends, or within communities—developing norms of helping each other grow, learn, and be open to new ideas would help us adapt to the ever-changing world. Such caring would also help build or maintain more resonant relationships, which, as we have explained, help the person offering the help as well as others by moving them periodically into the PEA. Although we are focusing the discussion in this chapter on work organizations, all of the points and examples would apply to creating a developmental culture in the other settings we mentioned as well.

bringing coaching to work organizations

Of course, coaching is still relatively new to organizations. Although coaching came to corporations in the late 1960s and early 1970s, it didn't become an established practice until the late 1990s and early 2000s. We are still exploring the many forms of coaching and finding ways to perfect it. One thing we've learned, however, is that the coaching relationship is key, especially when we consider that organizations are in need of resonant leaders who can motivate and engage others. We also know that coaching can elevate the professional prospects of certain special and at-risk groups in organizations, such as emerging leaders, minority groups, and women. This works in our families as well as with those feeling excluded or somehow marginalized.

For example, we know that in the United States, women in organizations don't receive coaching as much or as often as do men. Yet women "face distinct individual and organizational realities" that coaching could help them address, according to our friends and colleagues Margaret (Miggy) Hopkins, professor at the University of Toledo, and Deborah O'Neil, professor at Bowling Green State University. In one of our many discussions with Miggy and Deb, they noted that women remain underrepresented in leadership roles and are underpaid as a group. Coaching therefore could provide professional women with a safe place to contend with issues like career advancement in male-dominated fields and to reflect on work-life integration. They also found that researchers recommend coaching for helping both women and minorities find their unique voice and advance through organizational structures. You can see how similar dynamics might also be present in our families and communities.

But providing coaching isn't always easy, especially at first, as Jeff Darner found when he introduced coaching at Moen. And it can also be challenging even long after coaching has been introduced in an organization, as Niloofar Ghods discovered when she became leader of Cisco Systems' coaching practice. She walked into the job looking forward to providing a variety of development options for thousands of Cisco's executives and professionals. Little did she know that her first task would be taking stock of the deluge of coaching configurations already in place. Cisco was spending millions on coaching but could account for only a small percentage of the coaches being used by the company and its people. As Niloofar described it, "I had to clean house."[2]

We've heard the same story from many learning and development executives of *Fortune* 500 companies. Like Niloofar, they find they must begin by surveying and documenting how much coaching is being delivered and by whom. At that point, they review the best ways for people to have access to coaches. Moreover, ensuring consistent coaching quality and managing fees presents a major challenge, something Niloofar addressed by creating a training and certification process for all coaches Cisco uses, both internal and external.

But other organizations face development challenges that are far more complex than accounting for and providing the best coaching.

Amy Grubb coordinates staff development (which sometimes includes coaching) for twenty-five thousand people at the Federal Bureau of Investigation. Adding to the pressure of the job itself, FBI leaders are in the public spotlight daily. They have to present a veneer of perfection while somehow juggling the demands of truth, justice, and partisan politics. Although the FBI uses coaches automatically when onboarding a new executive or transitioning someone to a new job, Amy also created a program where a leader can request a coach as needed. When the federal budget became tighter, however, she began to encourage more "self-coaching" through mindfulness exercises.[3]

As these examples illustrate, creating an effective coaching culture requires a range of management skills and thoughtful discernment—everything from assessing overall need and managing access to coaches, to (sometimes) centralizing coach training and certification to ensure quality. We also see in these examples three basic approaches to offering coaching services in organizations: (1) encourage and train associates to peer coach in pairs or teams; (2) provide access to internal or external coaches (people professionally trained as coaches and typically certified by some professional group); and/or (3) educate and develop managers and senior leaders to provide coaching to their direct reports and others. In the remainder of this chapter, we will look at each of these three approaches in turn.

peer coaching

An approach used to craft a culture of coaching in organizations is peer coaching. It is also a beneficial way to introduce a norm of helping or coaching with compassion into families, teams, social groups, and even communities. This is an age-old process, of course; we used to call this "being friends." But many of us find we don't have much time today for talking directly to even our closest friends. Too often we rely on Facebook updates or texting or email at the expense of developing or maintaining deeper emotional relationships.

Peer coaching formalizes a personal, supportive connection for mutual help. The idea is for two or more people of relatively equal status to come together to help each other with personal and professional development, using a reflective process often involving recalling meaningful incidents or stand-out moments. Our colleagues Kathy Kram, Ilene Wasserman, Polly Parker, and Tim Hall describe the process of helping as dynamic and the main purpose of peer coaching "to promote goal-directed mutual learning with clear boundaries."[4] Reviewing specific events from work appears most helpful when the people involved see each of the events as a kind of living case study. So, one person selects an event of relative importance from work, presents it to the other individual or group, and together they brainstorm about how it went and what other options might have been available. This mode of review has been seen as more valuable when it involves peers talking to and helping one another, as opposed to peers being guided by an expert or "superior," which can feel like another level of the "ought" self being imposed, which then stimulates more NEA.

When more than two people are involved, then you have a peer-coaching group. One of the most successful peer-coaching groups to help people change their behavior is Alcoholics Anonymous.[5] It was the peer aspect—people stripped of formal status differences and talking as equals—that gave AA credibility. It enabled people to approach one of the most difficult behaviors to change, an addiction habit, with a sense of possibility. The members of a meeting, as they are called, come to rely on each other for insight, inspiration, and comfort. Knowing that they have each "been there" makes the discussions believable and honest.

Peer coaching can be formal or informal and can involve people from within and outside of the organization. These relationships often sustain themselves over long periods of time because the people develop deep, resonant relationships involving mutual caring and compassion, shared vision and purpose, and an upbeat, helpful mood.

Best of all, from an organizational standpoint at least, peer coaching offers a low-cost alternative for providing help to large numbers of managers and employees and can lead to a very positive cultural norm. In particular, peer coaching provides a great way for organizations to practice coaching on a daily basis and to cascade it down from managers to employees.

But how, exactly, does peer coaching work? Because peer-coaching groups tend to be durable and foster a meaningful way for peers or family members to relate to each other, the groups often stimulate the kind of positive emotional contagion that leads others, through social mimicry, to make positive changes. In this sense, peer-coaching groups can become a new form of support and in the best case, an extended family. All of this eventually leads to improved organizational norms. What's more, while peer coaching can be used to facilitate an organization's culture change, it sometimes turns out to be a crucial component to the culture itself. It can be more important than other forms of training, which can offer distractions and diversions to practicing coaching because of the other topics and participants. Peer coaching provides a dedicated social setting in which group members explore helping each other.[6]

Peer coaching can also take many formats. In the Case Western Reserve University courses, we ask people to develop their *personal board of directors*. This exercise not only helps people increase awareness of their key relationships and sources of support, but it also provides them with a ready-made list of people with whom they can check their progress. Our colleagues Monica Higgins and Kathy Kram call a similar formation *developmental networks*.[7] They recommend having a number of key people in the network and using them individually or together to continue exploring personal and professional growth.

In peer coaching, as with coaching delivered by a trained coach, relationships are key. All work in organizations occurs in a network, where each person is connected to others and where the actions of one impact someone else. When people work together in ways that are helpful, supportive, and meaningful through peer-coaching relationships, employees are given the support to innovate, adapt, perform, and even live healthier, more sustainable lives. In the safety net of trusting peer-coaching relationships, people exchange support, reality-test ideas, and interpret shared meaning of events. To be effective, participants need some form of self-awareness and reflection, as well as a great deal of caring and compassion for each other. (See the sidebar "Developing Your Coaching Skills in Organizations" and chapter 7 for more information on how to develop high-quality coaching relationships and refine your coaching skills.) Those elements are the emotional glue that facilitates intentional change and fosters learning. In contrast to task groups, the relationships and emotional bonds *are* the purpose of these groups. Our friends and colleagues Vanessa Druskat and Chris Keyes did a study of MBA learning teams and showed that norms that produced the highest grades (i.e., task performance) in a semester were almost opposite the norms that produced the most learning one semester later.[8] One example was that groups that received the highest grades (best task performance) avoided discussing conflicts, like uneven participation or freeloading (some people coasting on the work of others and not doing their fair share) among the team members. But those teams in which the MBAs felt they were *learning the most* openly discussed these and other conflicts and attempted resolutions, which in turn enabled them to perform better in the long run.

A word of caution: Sometimes peer coaching, especially peer-coaching groups, can turn to the "dark side" and focus on negative emotions. After all, that's how managers traditionally have been trained—to direct their attention on problem identification and problem solving. While this approach does help in some ways, it isn't very effective when it comes to human development. As we've shown throughout this book, a problem-focused approach may seem efficient, but it ignores the fact that thinking about and arousing feelings about problems activates the NEA, which in turn can close a person's imagination to new ideas and possibilities. Recognizing that a problem exists is quite different from spending a lot of time thinking and talking about it. It negatively frames the opportunity. As a result, people wallow in the mire of negativity and feel stuck as they sink further and further into the swill. To minimize the possibility of groups turning in a negative direction,

developing your coaching skills in organizations

The steps for developing coaching skills follow the stages of sustained, desired change as described in Intentional Change Theory:

1. First, examine your personal vision for your future and determine the extent to which helping others or coaching in any form is part of what you desire.

2. Once you develop a personal vision that includes coaching, take stock of your capability to establish effective helping relationships. For most people, participating in training is often helpful to expand understanding of the role of a coach and elevate your skills, whether you are a manager hoping to become a better coach of your team or a peer coach. This should ideally include regular assessment and feedback, and might involve face-to-face training, online courses (asynchronous like a MOOC or synchronous like a live, interactive webinar), or some combination of those options. If you aspire to become a professional coach, you'll need to invest in considerable training to develop the requisite skills.

it's a good idea for the group to periodically check in with a skilled coach or request specific training in group facilitation.

Once positive peer coaching becomes a norm within an organization, our friend and colleague Frank Barrett tells us, it "changes the social fabric."[9] Frank points out that to have and keep friends, we need "unscheduled time, repeated interaction, and a feeling of safety." He reminds us that Aristotle said that friends are the key to society.[10] The same is true in weaving a new social fabric. This changes what it means to be in the organization and in these relationships.

3. Identify professionals currently doing coaching in the manner you desire to learn, and then shadow the effective coaches or peer coaching groups. This is an important way to see coaching in action, and you can follow up your observation with a discussion with the coaches, sharing personal reflections.

4. The coaching process is composed of numerous elements or stages. This may include questions and actions that bring the coachee into the PEA rather than the NEA. Experiment, therefore, with aspects of the coaching process with which you are not familiar. Again, accompany each of your learning efforts with reflection and feedback from trusted others.

5. Follow your experimentation with practice that also includes reflection and feedback.

6. Repeat steps 4 and 5 until you achieve a degree of comfort and a sense of mastery.

new social identity groups

One of the many benefits of peer-coaching groups is that they often morph into what has been called a *social identity group*.[11] Take the case of one leadership program we studied, a group of twenty or so doctors, nurses, engineers, professors, and deans (many of whom held executive positions in their professions). In four longitudinal studies conducted one, two, and three years after they completed the program, they reported that along with major changes in their behavior and jobs, they had found with each other a new reference group. While most of the people they were closest to in their every-day lives wanted them to continue doing what they were doing—and often found discussion of major changes to be threatening—these participants told us that the group from the program remained the friends with whom they could talk about their dreams and futures.

This group evolved out of a highly innovative program, the Professional Fellows at the Weatherhead School of Management, which created an opportunity for advanced professionals with their terminal degree to continue developing. Using participative peda-gogy, the cohort met for a year, once a week, for a seminar in the evening, plus one Saturday each month for a more personal form of development. Participants created new personal vision statements and spent time learning to "coach" each other in converting their visions into learning plans for the next few years of their lives.[12]

Many executive programs and graduate degree programs report such spontaneous creations of social identity groups. Note that these relationships were not developed out of shared agony and tough experiences, like boot camps. As we have discussed about effective coaching relationships in earlier chapters, the PEA activi-ties helped them to come together and build deep understanding of each other's dreams. They cared about each other and their devel-opment. They had a shared vision, compassion, and level of energy. These resonant relationships had durability resulting from positive emotional contagion and shared purpose.

a tradition of peer coaching

Such peer-coaching groups, of course, are not new to organizations. In the 1960s and 1970s, peer-coaching groups were often called *support groups* or *T groups* (which stood for sensitivity training groups). In the 1980s, quality circles and other forms of employee participation groups became a popular trend. By the 1990s, this morphed into self-managing and self-designing work teams, and in the early 2000s people began experimenting with learning teams or study groups in organizations.

All of these forms had several things in common. First, they were informally generated, volunteer groups of peers. Second, their purpose was for the members to help each other with life, work, and learning (this was the main purpose, even if drinking and eating were a part of each meeting). Third, the members created their own agenda and managed their own process (i.e., no facilitators).

When a group gelled and people felt a rapport, it became a new social identity group for its members, who would look forward to their meetings. The relationships generalized beyond these meetings to other settings as people became friends and close colleagues at work. When the group members all worked in the same organization, others would observe their new ways of interacting outside of meetings. If the emotional contagion spread, new practices would turn into new norms in the organization.

Two forces combined to feed the growing energy that was driving peer coaching: *making coaching accessible* to a wider audience, not just executives, and *having a process that was enduring.* That is, the relationships and feelings generated in the group did not dissipate three to six weeks after the class, training program, or activity was completed, as is often the norm. It lasted! The accessibility of the coaching group enabled tens of thousands in an organization to benefit from coaching and development. And the company or government agency did not have to hire and pay hundreds of coaches or consultants.

We might think of expanding peer coaching as the ultimate developmental activity for organizations. It takes a focus on "the manager as coach" and extends it to every manager, professional, administrative, or production worker. This holds the potential for coaching to become a part of development for legions of people who might not normally have access to paid coaches. In this way, any associate can become a peer coach, spreading coaching throughout the entire organization. For individuals, a peer-coaching group can become their personal board of directors. Peer coaching, therefore, may hold the most promise of all approaches to build a culture of sustainable learning and development in organizations.

Indeed, one study shows that participating in such peer pairs during an MBA program led to people forming and using the pairs at work even many years later. The study, conducted by Parker, Kram, Hall, and Wasserman, provides the basis for a model for creating peer coaching within organizations, whether in pairs or small groups. First the pair forms a "holding environment" based on positive relationship building; next, it works on creating success by solving problems the participants are experiencing at work; and finally the fully formed peer-coaching pair—or combination of several pairs—grows into a small group that infiltrates the organizational culture, which in turn internalizes the peer-coaching skills and ethos. The researchers found that shared purpose is the medium that enables all of the stages in developing peer coaching.[13]

The sustainability of peer coaching plays out in many different forms. For example, a group of female partners of Coopers & Lybrand in the San Francisco Bay Area decided to get together monthly and talk about their lives and careers. They started with eight members and expanded to twelve. This informal group met for years, even with some members leaving and new ones joining. They sought out their peers (other female partners in a firm that had few at the time) to help each other. Their topics ranged from specific project advice to career counsel, and from personal help to sharing ideas about things of concern in the work environment. It was such a great example of peers helping each other that it was featured in a cover story in *BusinessWeek*.[14]

What's more, anyone who has successfully navigated graduate school, whether a medical or law degree, MBA, or PhD, knows that forming study groups and working together is a survival technique. We've seen firsthand how executive MBA programs often make learning possible through study groups, and that the executives report enjoying this activity. Traditional MBA students, on the other hand, often report that they hate working in teams, except in schools that target learning about working in teams like Case Western Reserve University. We believe this common attitude is because the traditional MBAs see working in a temporary team as a task to be accomplished and then moved on from (more AN, analytic network, focus, and NEA). Meanwhile, executive MBAs often work in the same study teams for all of their courses and the entire program. There is a benefit in the members learning to help each other and see their relationships as one of the purposes of the study team. It is not surprising, therefore, that many report having enjoyed working in teams.

If you've never experienced such a collegiate program, you've likely at least been exposed to the idea in feature films like *Legally Blonde* or TV series like *The Paper Chase* or *How to Get Away with Murder*. Lori Neiswander, an alum of our Masters in Positive Organizational Development program, reported forming just such a team with two classmates. Dubbing their group "Vino and Videos," they met on Friday nights with a bottle of wine and watched class-related assigned videos and discussed exercises and readings.

In programs seeking to build emotional and social intelligence, peer coaching is often used because the costs of hiring professional coaches is prohibitive for the programs. While one of us, Ellen, has been using peer coaching along with one-on-one individual coaching to enhance learning at Case Western Reserve University's emotional and social intelligence development course for MBA students, it is in the Engineering School that peer coaching became a major component of the course for undergraduates. Ellen provides brief training in coaching with compassion, with a focus on empathic listening, to the students, and she assigns them to peer-coaching trios. Students practice how to be a coach as well as experience what it feels like to benefit from a supportive, developmental relationship. A skilled mentor coach attends each of the trios' exercises and provides any guidance as needed.

Some peer-coaching groups survive and grow over decades. In 1974, Richard met with a study group of dental professionals in the Cleveland area to help with professional development. Twenty years later, after moving from Boston to Cleveland, they found him and met again with him. They had continued to meet, and the group is still going some forty-five years later. The study group has morphed to include social events with spouses, as well as professional development.

our new twist on peer coaching

We contend that the most powerful use of peer coaching will be with small groups of five to twelve people and using practices that invoke or elicit the PEA. As we have described earlier in this book, using activities and group norms that are more PEA will help the members be more open and feel the emotional encouragement that the group can provide. Note that it may require giving people some skill training in how to emphasize the positive emotional attractor.

When developing your own peer-coaching groups, we recommend that you start small. Carlos de Barnola Torres, Director of HR for the Iberian division of Covidien, said that his company started its peer coaching by asking people to find one other person and begin talking. Carlos emphasized gaining skills in asking questions and helping, not merely turning to a professional, internal coach to solve problems. After a while, he asked these pairs to find another pair. They formed quartets and continued the conversations. Soon, the coach could withdraw from the conversations and the quartets continued to meet and help each other. A new norm had been created at the company.

another approach: using internal and/or external coaches

Organizations looking to hire coaches first must decide whom to hire externally or internally, and sometimes companies choose to do both.[15] The internal option might begin with an internal training program on how to be a more effective coach. Many begin by contacting some form of coach-certifying body, which fall into two varieties. The most prevalent groups that provide a form of certification in coaching are universities and training companies that "certify" that a person has learned the institution's particular approach to coaching, its techniques, or method. These bodies seldom make claims beyond that. It is up to clients to determine if this certification adds value to their practice or capability as a coach. A selected few of these programs actually have published studies showing their impact, but most do not. Their evidence is based on referrals and usage by companies or government agencies (i.e., their client list).

The second group comprises associations or companies that "certify" that the person is a credible coach. This is a certification based on their group's competency model. Currently, the largest of these are the International Coach Federation (ICF), Worldwide Association of Business Coaches (WABC), and the Center for Credentialing and Education (CCE). The awkward issue is that there are no published studies showing which competencies or characteristics of particular coaches enable them to be more effective than others. That is, these associations and companies offer certification without any empirical evidence that their models actually work. Although they do research, it often takes the form of attitude or opinion surveys known in consulting circles as Delphi techniques in which current coaches claim what they think works. Unfortunately, such approaches have been shown repeatedly in other fields to create a standard of mediocrity and exclude certain groups.[16]

This leaves organizations with a dilemma. If they use existing certifications, it is not clear what they are ensuring. But they need some way to know whether someone is worth hiring. Perhaps the best method is to look for converging evidence from personal referrals, formal education, and certification in a variety of approaches. Using such methods to maximize quality of the coaches hired can help people seeking coaches to understand they are getting the best possible development, rather than simply being passed on to a "coaching call center" or a less competent team of coaches.

Internal coaches may also help when there's a unique circumstance that might take time to understand. For example, when the Cleveland Clinic, ranked as the number-two hospital in the United States, wanted to develop more of its physician leaders as general managers, it turned primarily to a cadre of internal coaches. The clinic, which was one of the largest US hospitals, had developed a highly effective patient-experience program that changed the culture. Meantime, it was acquiring other hospitals rapidly in many cities and several countries. While each of these aspects of the Cleveland Clinic was not unique, the combination created a situation that few professional coaches had encountered. The aggressive program of using coaches helped develop doctors, nurses, and staff as effective leaders. This expanded leadership pool enabled programmatic initiatives and growth in many areas.

developing managers to be coaches

Chris Baer, Vice President of Leadership Development and Talent Experience at Marriott International Learning and Development, took a different approach to creating a culture of coaching by developing managers as coaches. Specifically, he introduced a system of programs to "imbue managers with a coaching mindset to lead high-performing and adaptive teams."[17] Chris's objective was to shift managers' thinking to provide "developmental feedback in the moment, foster collaboration . . . and just-in-time professional development," among other things. The program involved training managers in coaching skills and creating peer-coaching support groups to encourage this new mindset. Chris and his colleagues believed this would be key to exceptional results in the emerging competitive business climate where change is constant.

This approach is not new. In the early 1970s, senior executives at Monsanto who worked in what we now call learning and development, asked coaching pioneer Walt Mahler to offer courses in coaching skills to selected executives.[18] Walt used his Coaching Practices Survey in a 360-degree format to collect information from the people these executives were trying to develop.

In the decades since then, learning and development staff at many organizations have tried to promote this coaching aspect of the manager's role more and more—primarily because managers themselves have become more focused on development as a reason to remain in a firm. In other words, managers, research has shown, wish to grow and advance through developing people in their organizations and have found that coaching is an effective way to do it.

Terry Maltbia of Columbia University's Coaching Certification Program feels strongly that the long-term future of organizations would be best served if all managers in any organization could become better coaches. The coaching program at Columbia uses his model of understanding the conditions, commitment, competence, and clarity for performance coaching, as the basis for teaching managers skills and perspectives on how to include coaching as part of their day-to-day responsibility.[19]

Of course, to ask managers to add coaching to their daily efforts means that they will need some training in why coaching is important in the first place and how to acquire both a coaching perspective and the skills required. The skills for developing others, as we have shown throughout this book, are not the same as typical management capabilities. One study showed how training managers in coaching skills improved sales of their entire teams.[20] Without such training, managers are likely to fall back on their personal views of others—biases that may be as basic as a belief that people can't change—which could interfere with how well they come across to others as caring and interested in others' development.[21]

This even can help in hospitals and health care. Dr. Patrick Runnels is not only a psychiatrist but also runs a fellowship program for doctors finishing their residency in psychiatry and working in community mental health sites. In a development program with coaching in which he was a participant, he experienced and practiced coaching with compassion. "It hadn't dawned on me that when giving feedback in supervisory settings," he said, "you can use coaching with compassion to reach more people." He was trying to prepare MDs who would be managing treatment teams to take a growth mindset and try to frame their work as not managing tasks but motivating people. During the program he was running for the fellows, he asked each to develop his or her personal vision. He had them practice coaching each other and then discuss it with peers, using coaching as a regular part of their supervision (or management) of others in the hospital. He even made the training into an experiment. He exposed half of the eleven fellows in the last cohort to the approach of coaching with compassion. The other half he did not. He paired them and asked them to try to motivate the other doctor through coaching. He said that during the plenary discussion after the exercise, the room was filled with excitement. Participants said coaching with compassion made a lot of sense *and* it was much more fun than typical ways people handle motivating others. Their reactions were, in his words, "amazing." Even though they were psychiatrists, he said, "Two-thirds had never thought of motivating others through the PEA." Now many of the fellows have put these methods into practice.

The larger strategic image is that if a critical mass of managers saw coaching as part of their day-to-day role—and did it—coaching would become a new norm rather than just an occasional practice. It could change an organization's culture to one that is more developmental and compassionate (i.e., caring), which seems more in tune with the largest group of employees in the emerging workforce, the millennials. According to international surveys, not only are millennials demographically as large if not larger than the baby boomers were; they are also more purpose driven and they seek development in their work.[22]

If managers, executives, leaders, and parents viewed coaching as part of their style—that is, their personal way of acting in their role—this would also contribute to a shift in an organization's and family's culture. Seeing coaching as part of your role instills an expectation that each manager or parent, teacher, doctor, or nurse should be coaching and helping others. That could possibly backfire because it adds another "ought" self to the helper. In our experience, however, the benefits outweigh the risk, and individuals enjoy and embrace the coaching role. And if the expectations are followed by a change in the helper's typical, day-to-day behavior, then it signals to anyone around them that coaching and developing others *is* a fundamental part of their job or role and appropriate behavior. When you change what people see as the rules of the game, how a person should act, and what they should value, you have changed the culture!

As Niloofar Ghods told us, since she arrived at Cisco, her company has changed the way coaching is delivered in an organization "in which disruption is a way of life. Positive psychology is an accelerant of coaching. But we have to democratize access and broaden the use. Technology will help." Niloofar is suggesting that with a technology company, with staff who are self-selected as technically oriented, finding ways to meet at a geographic distance but with high-definition quality (such as through Cisco's TelePresence or Webex Meetings) will make coaching across continents and the world an easier leap for them.

As authors, our hope and our vision are that as people begin to learn to coach each other with more PEA, they soon will start trying the same approach in their work units as well as in their families, friends, and acquaintances. Organizations will see the benefits daily, as will the people within them. With the benefit of emotional contagion, more and more peer-coaching groups will start meeting. Soon, a critical mass of the people in an organization will become involved in a peer-coaching process (*critical mass* is estimated as at least one-third of a group of people). Eventually, coaching with compassion will become a cultural practice or norm across organizations, and people will begin sharing stories globally of how they formed their peer-coaching groups. A veritable coaching revolution will have begun!

The reality, however, is that not everyone feels comfortable engaging in personal conversations about their dreams and building more resonant relationships. Sometimes individuals have difficulty accessing these thoughts and feelings. In chapter 9, we will explore how best to help reluctant participants.

key learning points

1. In families and other informal social groups, as well as communities, a culture of helping others develop and be open to learning would help us all adapt to an ever-changing world.

2. Creating an effective coaching/helping culture in work organizations requires careful assessment of need, centralized access to and allocation of coaches, and sometimes centralized coach training and certification to ensure quality.

3. There are three basic approaches to offering coaching services in organizations: (1) encourage and train staff to peer coach in pairs or teams; (2) train managers and executives to provide coaching to their direct reports and maybe even peers; and (3) provide access to internal or external coaches (people professionally trained as coaches and typically certified by some professional group).

4. A high-quality coaching relationship amplifies both job engagement and career satisfaction, and can be leveraged to help organizations develop and retain their best and brightest talent, especially among special and at-risk groups such as emerging leaders, minority groups, and women.

5. Peer coaching is simply the coming together of two or more people for the purpose of personal or professional development. It can be formal or informal, and within or outside a particular organization. The developmental purpose can supplement other reasons for the group existing.

6. Peer-coaching relationships blossom through caring, compassion, resonance, understanding, and shared purpose. They are durable, sustainable, and promote a positive emotional contagion that can become the basis of an organizational norm.

7. Be wary of peer-coaching relationships turning to the "dark side" and focusing primarily on the negative.

8. MBA programs that focus on team learning and relationships demonstrate tangible benefits beyond the education phase itself. A proactive focus on peer coaching can pay for itself down the line by enhancing the integration of learning for each member.

9. Peer-coaching groups promote an intimate involvement among all members of the group, which results in enduring social bonds outside the organization. Evidence suggests that such groups can create and consolidate a healthy collective identity.

conversation guide

1. In groups, discuss when you have seen coaching used in leadership development in an organization.

2. Describe to others the benefits individuals and the organization derived from the coaching or developmental experiences. Examine the outcomes of the coaching impact, if any.

3. Examine with others how coaching might be leveraged in your organization or with clients to help at-risk populations. Further examine how such coaching might help at-risk members of your families or other informal social groups.

4. Discuss whether or not your organization formally or informally uses peer coaching in small groups. What could you do to start or expand peer coaching?

5. Describe to others who your main peers are both at and outside of work. Who are the people with whom you feel a social bond?

6. Explore with others any informal or formal groups of which you are a member that get together and discuss life and work. How often do you meet? Describe the interactions and discussions. Are they predominantly PEA or NEA? Are they helpful to you or others? Have they helped you or others change jobs or improve performance at work?

recognizing coachable moments

seize the opportunity

Fall had arrived. The air was cool and crisp, and the trees were turning from green to bright yellow, orange, and red. For Ray Lewis, however, this fall was more than just a change of season; it was also a time of transition in his life. Ray had decided to embark on an educational and personal development journey that would prepare him for the next big step in his career—to assume greater responsibility in his family's business.

That path had been laid out for Ray for many years. Already he was serving as corporate accounts manager for the company his family founded in 1989 to provide planned and emergency response services, including spill cleanup, environmental remediation, and transportation of waste. Ray's father was part owner of the company, and he'd long been grooming Ray to play a more prominent role.

Not only was Ray's professional future laid out for him, certain aspects of his personal future had been prescribed as well. For example, when the family decided to sell the home where Ray and his siblings had spent their childhood, they convinced Ray to help keep it in the family by buying it and investing money in its needed renovation.

All of this would have been fine—except that deep down, Ray knew he wanted something else, although he didn't know exactly what that was. Fortunately, the executive MBA program in which Ray had enrolled, which included personal coaching, was designed to help him reflect on and articulate a personal vision for his future.

When Ray began working with his coach, he admitted that advancing in the family business felt flat and somewhat constraining. Yet the coach saw that Ray still seemed willing to fulfill the career path that had been carefully crafted for him (with loving intentions) by others. The "ought" self can be especially powerful when family relationships get mixed with professional work. Although he was eager to learn and grow, Ray hadn't fully appreciated the power of identifying and pursuing his true passion.

That is the essence of what we call a *coachable moment.* For the coach, manager, teacher, or other helper, identifying a coachable moment comprises two aspects: (1) observing a critical situation or learning opportunity that the individual may or may not be aware of; and (2) correctly perceiving that the individual is open and ready for reflection and learning around that opportunity.

In this chapter, we'll look at more examples of coachable moments and then how to determine if a person is actually ready to be coached. We'll provide a practical guide for creating a safe space for reflection and openness, and we'll discuss typical "tough" coaching cases and how the techniques of coaching with compassion can help.

coachable moments all around us

Ray's situation came to light within a formal coaching relationship, but when we pay attention, we can see coachable moments in many scenarios around us. The senior leader who has been "invited" to take a promotion that will mean he'll be traveling three out of four weeks every month and who is concerned about the toll that will take on his relationships with his wife and kids. The friend who feels a calling to start a nonprofit organization to help disadvantaged high-school students gain access to higher education—but who's reluctant to quit her lucrative corporate career to pursue that calling. The employee struggling in his new supervisory role who now realizes he accepted the promotion primarily because of his family's ideas about "career advancement." The diabetic patient who refuses to adhere to his treatment protocol even though he knows there will be dire health consequences. The high-school senior who's been accepted at several top universities, but who is unsure about what she wants to do in life and is thinking of taking a gap year and traveling around Europe before starting college. Or any one of the many professional women who left the workforce to raise children and years later feel lost as to how to jumpstart the return to a career.

But there are other key moments too. One major time when people are open to coaching and help is when they're taking on a new position, according to research by our friend and colleague Claudio Fernández-Aráoz. He found that the first two years in the job is a critical time to help someone be more effective.[1] Claudio is tapping into a more general category of coachable moments— times of life or career transition. Additional examples of coachable moments might include an upcoming graduation, new job, first home purchase, getting married, having or adopting a baby, being laid off or fired, hitting the lottery, getting an inheritance, or being diagnosed with a lifelong or terminal illness. There may be other transition moments that might not seem as earthshaking as the above list, but they are all opportunities for individuals to rethink their personal dreams and visions for the future. In an earlier chapter, we referred to life and career cycles that also create such moments.

When we fail to recognize coachable moments, we miss the chance to help others. We don't do this intentionally, of course; in the midst of our own hectic schedules and daily stresses, it's easy to miss key moments in a colleague's or family member's life. Or perhaps we feel that we can't be helpful because we haven't experienced what the person is going through and don't have suggestions to offer. Even if we recognize a coachable moment, however, we'll likely fall short of truly helping the individual if we don't respond to it effectively. And, as with many things in life, sometimes timing and readiness are key.

recognizing readiness

Whether a coachable moment is associated with a broader, long-term change effort or a more narrowly defined issue or opportunity an individual is facing, the person needs to be ready to be coached or else the impact will be far less meaningful. Bruce Avolio and Sean Hannah have studied readiness in the field of leadership development, which we can apply to coaching readiness as well. They found that when companies target employees for leadership, sometimes they need to assess and enhance, if necessary, the developmental readiness of those individuals.[2] Likewise, before trying to help someone through a coachable moment, coaches or other helpers should assess and if possible, enhance, the coaching readiness of the individual.[3]

The model of change developed by James Prochaska and his colleagues stresses the importance of readiness to an individual's change efforts. This model has been widely adopted in the fields of psychotherapy and executive coaching and consists of five stages, the first three of which (pre-contemplation, contemplation, and preparation) describe levels of readiness.

In the pre-contemplation stage, individuals are clearly not yet ready to change; the need or desire to change is not even on their radar. In the contemplation stage, they still aren't quite ready to change, but they are at least thinking about it and trying to get themselves ready to do so. It is not until they reach the preparation stage that they are truly ready to change, however. Until individuals reach this stage of readiness, they are unable to effectively move on to the action and maintenance stages of change (the fourth and fifth stages in the model, where change is actually made and sustained).[4]

responding to a coachable moment

We sometimes respond to coachable moments by treating them as problems to be solved. As a result, we offer advice or solutions rather than coaching. While this may seem to be an effective way of helping at that time, it is less likely to lead to learning and growth for the individual involved. It is just not sustainable. The difference between advice and coaching is nicely expressed by the aphorism, "Feed a man a fish so that he can eat today; teach him to fish so that he can eat for a lifetime." Another example is that of a teenager who has just been told a valuable "life lesson" from his parents—but he promptly forgets because he hasn't experienced the situation himself.

As coaches and professors who advise PhD students who are typically in their thirties, we can add that when we give in to the urge to offer advice, the advisee sometimes (if not often) ignores it. But when we're able to recognize and take advantage of coachable moments in ways that inspire a student's growth and curiosity, that's when we, as advisers, truly become coaches.

Coaching with compassion is how we help a person frame the situation or opportunity in the context of who she wants to be as a person and what she would like to achieve in her ideal future. Such broad framing helps the person draw on the inner resources most likely to enable her to learn, change, or grow in meaningful and sustained ways as she works through that situation, whatever it may be.

Remember too that coachable moments may also take the form of something smaller in scale that doesn't necessarily involve a career or life decision. (See the sidebar "Recognizing Micro-Coachable Moments.")

recognizing micro-coachable moments

Perhaps a coworker is having a difficult time dealing with a particular member of your department. The relationship has become strained and dysfunctional and she doesn't know what to do to improve the situation. Or maybe a good friend, who was a standout athlete in college, shares with you that his son (who is also a star athlete) wants to quit the high-school football team to focus his time and energy on acting with the school's drama club and local community theater groups. After letting his emotions get the best of him and having an explosive outburst at his son—expressing considerable disappointment, frustration, and anger—he now regrets it and wants to figure out how to get back on track with him.

While such coachable moments might not involve as deep and comprehensive an application of the intentional change process as we have described thus far, as a coach you could still help the individual by applying the process on a smaller scale. For instance, in the example of the coworker with the strained relationship, you could ask her what an ideal relationship with the department member would look like.

challenging coaching cases

As we have discussed throughout this book, coaching with compassion generally leaves the person being coached feeling excited, energized, and ready and able to pursue sustained change. Most people welcome the opportunity to be coached in this way. After all, who wouldn't want someone to help them articulate and then pursue their dreams of an ideal future? However, sometimes helping someone can be difficult, even when you are coaching with compassion. Next, we explore five typically challenging kinds of coaching situations. Although the examples we offer here are all from professional coaching cases, the lessons are the same for

You could then have her think about the history of their interactions (from both her own and others' perspectives) that led to the current state of affairs. Next, you could have her think of possible strategies to improve the strained relationship with this person. What has she tried in the past? What new approaches might she try going forward? Finally, you could encourage her to reach out to other friends and/or coworkers besides you, who might also support her efforts to improve the strained relationship.

While these are essentially the same steps you would take in coaching someone over time through the entire intentional change process, we can see how the process can also be applied in "micro-cycles" in response to specific coachable moments. It applies a similar logic but in a more narrowly focused way than the grander scale of a personal life vision and purpose. Ideally, however, such smaller cycles should be consistent with and support the broader pursuit of the person's ideal self and personal vision. And, the main purpose is still to help people into the PEA so they can be open to new ideas and possibilities.

anyone—managers, teachers, parents, and so on—trying to help another person change. Reviewing these cases should better enable you to handle them, or similar cases, should you encounter them.

satisfied with life just as it is

Many years ago, when Melvin was just starting out as a coach using intentional change theory and the coaching with compassion approach, he ran into a case that really stumped him. In the short time he'd been coaching with compassion, he'd come to think of it as "liberation coaching." He was amazed at how freeing it was for individuals to frame the coaching engagement, and what they hoped to get out of it, in the context of what they truly wanted to do with the rest of their lives. Tapping into their passions, dreams, and deepest aspirations as the overarching frame for their desired change efforts was transformative for many individuals. And even in the cases where it wasn't necessarily transformational, it seemed to at least be an energizing, positive emotional experience for almost everyone he coached in this way—at least, until he met Anjit Singh (not his real name).

At fifty-three years old, Anjit had successfully moved through significant positions in quality control, manufacturing operations, and IT in a major US chemical company. Anjit and his wife Indira, to whom he had been married more than thirty years, had three children who were now grown, successfully building careers and lives of their own.

While most people Melvin coached found it fun and exciting to reflect on exercises designed to help them craft their ideal self and personal vision, Anjit found the exercises difficult and of limited value. From his perspective, he had a job that he loved, and he had a wife, family, and overall life that he loved even more. What was there to dream about? There was really nothing in his life that he wanted to change.

Having coached some individuals who were initially hesitant to allow themselves to dream about an ideal future in an unconstrained fashion, Melvin kept encouraging Anjit to allow himself to think about an ideal view of the *next* phase of his life—even if he was incredibly happy with where things were today. Still no movement from Anjit. He saw no value in envisioning something else other than what he was currently experiencing.

Melvin was puzzled and wondered if he were doing something wrong. Why couldn't he find the "magic questions" to open Anjit up to the exciting possibility of envisioning even more for his life than he'd already experienced?

That's when Melvin asked his mentor Richard for help; surely, he had the silver bullet that would open Anjit up to some desired change he wished to make in his life. But what Richard said surprised him: for some individuals, the ICT process is not about making a desired change to *achieve* an ideal self. Instead, for some it is about *sustaining* or maintaining an ideal self already achieved. That was an enlightening moment for Melvin as a coach: the ICT process does not always have to be about making change. If someone has already achieved a desirable life, unless and until that image of his ideal self changes, the process can be more about doing things that will support and maintain that ideal life.

Melvin shifted his approach with Anjit, and it clicked. Now Anjit could embrace the intentional change process as something more than just an exercise that had no real value to him. Instead he could begin to envision ways to solidify and sustain the wonderful life that he had already created. He was able to articulate a vision and develop a plan to ensure that he was prepared to deal with any potential factors that could impact his ability to sustain the ideal life he had achieved.

living in a repressive or oppressive environment

In 1996, the Weatherhead School of Management received a grant to offer top executives from a number of Russian companies advanced techniques and ideas in modern management and leadership. One participant in the six-week program was Julia (not her real name), the CFO of one of the largest engineering manufacturing organizations in Russia. Richard was her coach in the program.

Walking into the management building on the third morning of the program, Richard saw Julia and smiled, asking how she was doing.

She grimaced and said, "Awful. I was so upset that I could not sleep." Richard said he was sorry to hear that and asked what had upset her. She turned to him and said, "You!"

Richard, who thought that the seminar and discussions had gone well, was shocked. He asked, "What was it I said or did that was so upsetting?" By then, they had reached the lobby and Richard suggested they get a coffee and talk.

When they sat down with their coffee, Julia explained:

> I am forty-two. I grew up professionally in our company and advanced rapidly. The leaders liked what I could deliver and how I managed. But I have never been asked or allowed to *dream*. Up until a few years ago, it was assumed that the top leadership or party officials would tell you what your next job was. That was it. As a matter of fact, if you dreamed about conditions in a desirable future that criticized the present, you could be turned in to the authorities as being seditious, with severe consequences (e.g., being sent to the Gulag). So you settle into the expectation that dreaming of better possibilities is a bad thing to be avoided.

At this point, Julia was hanging her head. Richard waited before she added, "It feels like such a waste of talent—all those years and decades. I don't know if I can change sufficiently to even create a personal vision."

Although Julia's example was extreme, there are many refugees fleeing countries under conditions of war or religious, economic, political, or psychological oppression who have trouble once free. In his classic analysis, Viktor Frankl documented how he and many Holocaust escapees and survivors had difficulty for years in their new home countries because their existence was entirely focused on surviving or their family surviving. During the process, many lost hope repeatedly.[5]

In Julia's case, she would be leaving the program to return to a dramatically changed environment but with her old beliefs and ways of dealing with management issues. The way to handle this coachable moment, then, was to reduce her anxiety and focus on what kind of person she wanted to be. By helping her focus less on what she hoped to *do* and more on her values—who she wanted to *be* and how she acted with others—Richard was able to help Julia focus on something within her control. Julia's values were uniquely her own; reflecting on them allowed her to return to her authentic self, which was both grounding and liberating.

When working with people whose environments are restrictive, the best approach is to focus on their core values—those beliefs about what is right, good, true—which are fundamental to being, living, and if appropriate, leading authentically. From that foundation, they can often consider behaviors and actions that can be seen, altered, and experimented with day-to-day in support of their values. That is often more feasible than framing a ten- to fifteen-year personal vision.

torn between equally attractive and mutually exclusive ideals

Joseph (not his real name) had just gotten his dream job as CEO of a midsized company. He wanted to advance even further, however, so he was completing a doctorate at the same time. He had used visioning and planning his whole life and had even taught the process as an adjunct professor to MBA students. Joseph had outlined stages in his coming years with the priorities shifting at each stage. In his current stage, he wanted to be a better father and husband, as well as a better human being to everyone with whom he interacted in contributing to his community. He wanted less stress in his life and to be more mindful.

Joseph had three dreams. One was to build the company and show how effective leadership can work. The second was to lead a more balanced life and spend quality time with his family, friends, and others. His third dream was to write, publish, teach, and be a public speaker who motivated others to reach for their dreams.

The dilemma was that he could not feasibly accomplish all of those at the same time. The time and energy demands of running and growing a business were, on the whole, incompatible with a more balanced, less-stressful lifestyle. His coach tried the one thing that often works with people with multiple dreams, some of which appear to be incompatible. The coach asked Joseph to prioritize his dreams—literally, to rank order them. "If you could only do one of these, which one would you want to do the most?" Joseph knew that it was to be with his family more. But he had led a driven life and work style. So the coach asked, "Which of the other two could allow you to spend more time with your family than you do now and still pursue that work dream?"

Like getting hit by a bolt of lightning, it became clear to Joseph that he needed to make a specific plan to transfer leadership of the company within two years. Before that happened, he was able to begin publishing and giving lectures at various universities. He tried to include his family on more of his work trips, planned more vacation and relaxation time with them, and promised that after the CEO job was finished, he would devote a great deal of his time to his wife and children. Within two years, as he completed his doctorate, he had transferred ownership of the consulting company and explored faculty positions. He was hired as a tenure-track professor at a university that emphasized teaching and not the publish-or-perish race he wanted to avoid and that would threaten progress on his other ideal—spending time with his family. Today, a number of years have passed, and Joseph reports he has succeeded. But he could not have gotten to this point without confronting and reprioritizing his aspirations.

too much invested in the current path
to change direction now

Gabriela (not her real name) was a prosecutor in a midsized US city. She was intrigued with how coaching might work and agreed to meet with a personal coach—but that was about the limit of her willingness to explore possibilities.

When the coach asked her about her dreams of a perfect life, she looked at her watch and said, "This is too self-serving." The coach understood that she didn't feel positive about her future possibilities, but what he didn't know was just how hesitant that made her about even talking about it. The coach asked about her ideal image of work. Her response focused on resolving present workload issues. He asked about her dream of an ideal personal life. She said she didn't have time for one.

Gabriela had come from a working-class family and was the first to go to college. She was also the first to attend graduate school and become a professional. With a highly prestigious government job, Gabriela had achieved more than she had ever thought possible as a young woman. She did it by working harder than anyone else around her. She had sacrificed when friends were having fun. She had devoted herself to her work in ways that others thought a bit single-minded.

But she had made it. Gabriela was now middle-aged and knew she'd paid a price for her success: she had missed out on having a family and enjoying the kinds of personal relaxation she knew others had. This wasn't intentional. It had just happened that way. She had always focused on her career and hadn't put the same focus and energy into dating and activities outside of work. Yet she felt comforted by the knowledge that none of her friends had gotten as far as she had, both professionally and socially.

Her coach tried many different approaches to get her to consider what she wanted out of life and to explore possibilities for the future. All she could see was the present. Although at some level, she may have felt trapped, she literally did not allow herself to think about it. It had taken too much to get to this point, and she was not going to give it up! For Gabriela, the coaching did not translate into new learning, new insights, or new behaviors. Perhaps at some point in the future, she'll have an awakening of some kind, after a crisis or other kind of transition, and be ready to engage in the process. But this was clearly not that time for her.

Another variation of someone not ready or willing to be coached is when the person goes along to "play the game." This happened to one of our colleagues, who tried to help a former coachee, Franklin (not his real name), who had just been released from prison and was out on parole. Although they had an engaging initial conversation, Franklin's coach walked away unsure anything would happen as a result. With a history of multiple convictions and even more arrests, Franklin's past did not offer a lot of hope. But his coach knew he'd started a driving service, and he'd gotten a job as caretaker for a local community center—so he had at least a fighting chance to succeed this time.

The challenge was that Franklin couldn't see anything beyond his current tasks. He had not a long-range dream but rather a short-term plan—staying out of jail and having some form of legal employment. While the typical "coaching to a long-range vision" method did not seem to help or even engage him, he at least was willing to discuss his steps and intention of staying compliant with the conditions of his parole and making a life for himself.

That's when his coach shifted his focus from the future to the present. "How do you wish to be acting and to be seen by others now—this week, next month?" the coach asked. That engaged Franklin. Like many people with biochemical or behavioral habits that are addictive and that simply recreate the conditions that got them in trouble, people in these situations are fighting against the odds of recidivism and their own past. By focusing on the present, Franklin was able to work with the coach to find new social groups and develop a new identity to make a sustainable change in his life. Besides building his new business, he wanted to be seen as someone who was trustworthy, reliable, and approachable. Reflecting with his coach on this identity he desired gave his life new meaning.

trapped in an "ought" self

Recall our opening story of Ray Lewis. He proved to be a challenging case for his coach. Here was a situation where the coachee knew that he wanted to do something other than what he was doing currently. But he was having a hard time envisioning and articulating what that might be, and an even harder time imagining how he could possibly pull away from the path that had been so clearly established for him.

Ray's coach, however, could almost see another version of Ray, inside of a shell trying to break out—but that shell of his "ought" self was seemingly impenetrable. His coach tried a number of ways to help Ray imagine what a self-defined view of his ideal future might look like, but Ray was so clear on what his father wanted for him that he couldn't craft his own vision. And because he loved his father dearly and didn't want to disappoint him, Ray felt truly trapped.

Throughout their relationship, Ray's coach continued to challenge him to examine and then follow his heart. Eventually, Ray decided that it was time to take a bit of a leap. He could no longer suppress the desire he felt to explore a life of his own choosing. Ray took a leave of absence from work and spent some time traveling the world. During his travels, he reflected on who he wanted to be and what he really wanted to do with his career and life. It was during these travels that things finally clicked for Ray: he knew what he wanted to do and how he was going to go about doing it.

Sometime after his return, Ray attended an executive MBA alumni function. He immediately approached his coach and confidently shook his hand, saying, "Hi. Meet Ray Lewis." Ray had finally found himself. He had discovered his ideal self and, with it, the passion and confidence to pursue it. He now knew in his heart what he wanted for his future. With his newfound passion and confidence, Ray soon left the family business and cofounded a small business of his own. Since that moment when he was able to escape the grip of what felt like a constraining "ought" self to pursue his own ideal vision, Ray has flourished both personally and professionally. His relationship with his father (who eventually understood and respected Ray's decision) is as strong as ever, and he is living life with a newly found sense of joy and adventure.

Recognizing coachable moments so that we can effectively capitalize on them and being able to handle challenging cases in addition to the "easy" ones are important for coaches, managers, and anyone else trying to help another person. Our approach of coaching with compassion, and the various nuances we have discussed in this book, should equip you to do both of these things well. In chapter 10, we offer final words of inspiration to prepare you to go forth and, we hope, apply the things you have learned in this book as you help others through coaching conversations that inspire them.

key learning points

1. A coachable moment involves a potentially critical situation or learning opportunity of which the person to be coached may or may not be fully aware, *and* the coach correctly perceives that the individual is both open and ready for reflection and learning around that situation or opportunity.

2. Capitalizing on coachable moments often involves assessing and potentially enhancing the readiness of the individual to be coached. If an individual is not ready to be coached, the extent of their coaching-facilitated change is likely to be limited.

reflection and application exercises

1. Think about the last time you encountered someone who was in the midst of what we have described in this chapter as a *coachable moment*. Did you recognize and treat it as a coachable moment? How did the person respond? Was she ready to be coached? Is there anything that you would have or could have done differently in your handling of the situation to be most helpful?

2. What are some of the more challenging cases that you have encountered as a coach, manager, teacher, parent, cleric, or other person who was trying to help someone? How might you apply some of the lessons learned from this book to help you in the future more effectively deal with those situations?

conversation guide

1. What ideas or techniques from this book are you eagerly looking forward to trying and developing further?

2. Are you finding coachable moments in one aspect of your life and work, but not others? How can you become sensitive to such moments in the other aspects of your life?

the call of compassion

an invitation to dream

Most of us care about others and try to help them. The source of our caring may be a desire to inspire people with whom we work to learn and grow or to protect our children or others. It might also be a desire to help others improve their performance or live up to their potential. It might reflect a deeper sense of love. All of these desires are noble but can easily lead us to do the exact opposite of what we intend. We can quickly slide into trying to fix others or prescribing specific ways to change. Although it may seem more efficient, by this point in the book we hope you recognize this slip into wanting to fix others as coaching for compliance (however well intended) and a catalyst for negative emotion and stress.

As leaders, parents, teachers, doctors and nurses, and coaches of all kinds, we are all witnesses to the reality show called "Life." We see injustice and people treated poorly around us. We are offended at people who feel entitled to "free stuff" and abuse the kindness of strangers. But most of all, we see people in influential roles seeming to promote themselves more than helping or leading others.

In a world of rampant narcissism and self-righteous, self-centered thinking (after all, this is the generation of selfies as a popular form of photography and social media!), we can do our part to reduce defensive behavior by helping others and building better relationships. The best antidote to self-centered narcissism is to care for others. One genuine way that you, the reader, can help others is to inspire and motivate them toward the best version of themselves. The positive emotional contagion created in the process will also help you feel inspired and positively influence others around you. Compassion is contagious!

In the earlier chapters, we asked you to reflect on who helped you the most to become who you are or to get to where you are in life. We explored how people's answers to that question show us how compassion through gratitude invokes the PEA and all of the good things that come with it. So let us now ask you a follow-up question: Whose list will *you* be on? It may be our most enduring legacy in life—making a difference in other people's lives.

compassion as an antidote to self-centeredness

Through the real-life stories of people becoming energized by the possibility of a new future, we hope you have a new appreciation for how and why connecting positively and deeply with others is beneficial both for your own personal sustainability and those with whom you interact in the multiple arenas of your life. We contend, based on our research, that the one powerful and accessible way to care for and help others is to coach with compassion. Not every conversation presents a coachable moment and coaching in the way we've suggested is not the only way. Coaching for compliance is needed at times, and in small doses. But too often, we let the NEA dominate the experience and therefore shorten the durability and limit the sustainability of any learning or change. Coaching with compassion is something we can all do with intention and practice as the stories throughout were meant to illuminate. Here are some highlights.

The Greg Lakin, Emily Sinclair, and Amy Szabo stories (chapters 1, 2, and 6, respectively) showed us how dramatic the impact on people's lives can be when we coach with compassion in contrast to coaching for compliance. That is, great helpers and coaches inspire, encourage, and support others in the pursuit of their dreams and the achievement of their full potential. In each of these cases, coaching with compassion began by helping them explore and clearly articulate their ideal self and a personal vision for the future, and tease out the distinction between their ideal self and ought self. As we saw in Mary Tuuk's case (chapter 5), a personal vision was a holistic, comprehensive expression of her ideal self and ideal future, including dreams, sense of calling, passion, purpose, and core values. The vision provides meaning in life and work. It helped each of them continue on the fruitful, but often frustrating, path to getting closer to their ideal self.

As we saw in Neil Thompson, Darryl Gresham, and Sean Hannigan's stories (chapters 2, 4, and 7, respectively), key resonant relationships helped them make a leap and move forward. Because emotions are contagious, the quality of the relationship with the helper or coach is crucial to inviting the PEA repeatedly. Beyond the relationship to the helper or coach, a person is more likely to sustain their learning and change efforts if they develop a network of trusted, supportive relationships. Lori Neiswander's example (chapter 8), showed how helping others to form peer coaching groups can feel like simply the coming together of two or more people for the purpose of personal or professional development. But the quality of the relationships is durable and helps the change effort be sustainable while promoting a positive emotional contagion, which can become the basis of an organizational or family norm.

As we saw in Aaron Banay's story (chapter 4), asking someone an evocative, open, positive question can elicit new information. We know from research that it awakens the PEA, activating a specific network in the brain that triggers hormones called the *parasympa-*

thetic nervous system (i.e., renewal). Asking a negative question or questions pulls a defensive response and arouses the NEA, activating a different network in the brain, which triggers hormones that are the *sympathetic nervous system* (i.e., stress). In Melvin's story (chapter 3), such questions activated the ought self, narrowed the possibilities, and made him feel stuck.

In Ellen's health story (chapter 6), we saw that entering the PEA is both a state of being open to new ideas *and* a tipping point along the path of sustained, desired change. We know from others' research and our own neuroimaging studies that to sustain a change or learning process, a person needs to regularly cycle into the PEA two to five times more often than being in the NEA. We saw further in Bob Shaffer's story (chapter 5) that renewal activities in smaller doses—in terms of time and more frequent episodes of renewal activities—are better than longer, less frequent ones. It also revealed that renewal using a variety of activities is better than using the same one or two repeatedly.

We witnessed in Melvin's story how focusing on strengths and not weaknesses in the context of his personal vision opened new possibilities. He experienced a profound sense of freedom and purpose as a result. The process of change often unfolds in discrete steps, such as in Sean Hannigan's experience to become a better leader by becoming a better listener. Other ways to invite the PEA include envisioning an exciting future and creating a plan that was energizing not obligatory, as we saw in Bassam's story of change to becoming a more patient and friendly project leader (chapter 6).

Entering the PEA and coming back to it during conversations often requires a resonant relationship and the feeling of care and trust that comes with it. We saw that build in Karen Milley's story of talking to her son (chapter 6). She then transferred her experience to create different conversations with direct reports at work. As we saw in Ellen's story of the conversations with her teenage daughter (chapter 7), high-quality helping relationships require helpers to prepare their mindset to create a positive, meaningful connection through deep, active listening. This is fundamental and essential for coaching with compassion.

Ellen's story of conversations with her daughter also showed how a coachable moment requires the coach or helper to be prepared to notice when such a moment is happening and adopt a coaching mindset. It involves a potentially critical situation or opportunity to which the person to be coached may or may not be fully aware, *and* the coach correctly perceives that the individual is both open and ready for reflection and learning around that situation or opportunity. Capitalizing on coachable moments often involves assessing and potentially enhancing the readiness of the individual to be coached.

We referred throughout the book to a number of organizations that use coaching. But we also illustrated how coaching can benefit families and a long list of other helping relationships. There are three basic approaches to making positive helping a norm in your families, communities, and at work. They are: (1) encourage (and/or train as needed) people to coach each other (at work this would be peer coaching in pairs or teams); (2) provide access to a variety of internal or external kinds of coaches or helpers; and/or (3) equip managers, physicians, and other helpers in positions of influence to build developmental relationships and provide coaching to those within their team and organization.

learn to help yourself

Even with the best of intentions, people cannot inspire and help others to learn and grow when they slip into the NEA themselves. The personal sustainability of the helper or coach is central to the ability to continue effectively helping others be open, develop, and change.

Our recommendation is straightforward but sometimes difficult to implement amid the stressors of everyday life and work. The key is to dose yourself with renewal every day. It is, in fact, the responsibility of helpers or coaches to sustain themselves and emote the positive emotional contagion that can only come from experiencing the PEA more than being in the NEA. In other words, we suggest that it is not a self-centered act to make sure you have renewal moments each day. Helpers and coaches looking to develop a long-term, sustainable means of reaching and maintaining a level of effectiveness would benefit from forming peer-coaching groups with other coaches. Coaches of all kinds need support just as much as the people they are trying to help and support.

an invitation to dream

A primary theme we've stressed throughout this book is using a personal vision to evoke positive emotions—essentially, to begin with the end in mind, thereby setting up the connections in the brain and emotions that will help us pave the road to the desired end. So now, we invite you to dream with us for a moment.

Imagine it is ten to fifteen years from now. If you are:

> *A coach:* You have many, many clients and they come from a variety of cultures. Your clients are transforming, learning, growing, developing, and performing. They are living meaningful lives. Most of all, they are thriving emotionally, physically, spiritually, and relationally. Some clients have formed peer-coaching groups, and in some of your clients' organizations, peer-coaching groups have become a norm. What's more, there is evidence that in your clients' organizations, the cultures are becoming more engaging and developmental than they've ever been.

> *A manager:* Your people are excited and engaged in their work. They feel a shared sense of purpose. They are innovating and adapting to changing market conditions and customers' needs. They feel that you are connected to the needs of people and are committed to their development. You invest in their growth and advancement. You provide exciting and novel projects. Your people not only want to stay in your organization, but also wish they had more time to spend at work. They are so excited that they've formed peer-coaching

groups in which they reality test, help each other deal with problems, and envision a better future. In fact, the entire company culture has changed, with everyone contributing to one another's development.

A physician, nurse, or physician assistant: You have motivated others to achieve wellness. Your role is to help people truly heal and maintain health, and your patients' adherence to their treatment plans are at 100 percent. Patients get better faster and stay well longer. All of this occurs because they take care of themselves. They are vulnerable to fewer maladies, with a high quality of life and low health-care costs. If your work is in palliative care, your patients leave this life with dignity, feeling loved and at peace.

A parent: Daily events in your home life feel like an idealized movie version of a loving and caring family. Your teenage children want to talk to you. Meals with the family involve interesting conversations and laughter. When anyone in the family needs advice, they come to you. Your older children take you out to dinner periodically, and you are involved in family vacations with your children and their families.

A therapist, counselor, pastoral counselor, or social worker: Your clients are focused on well-being—beyond their problems. They want to be well and are motivated to carry out their therapy or treatment plans. They spend less time egocentrically focusing on themselves and more time helping others less fortunate in the community. They care for others and extend themselves. They engage their families in loving and fun activities and strive to improve their work organizations.

Sound good? Here's a way to make such visions more likely to happen, for anyone reading this book. It's kind of a "pay it forward" experiment we can all try. Next month, each day have just *one* fifteen- to twenty-minute conversation with a different person to help them discover and connect with the best version of themselves, their values, dream life, desired work, or personal vision.

It may sound daunting, but it is likely that you will work or interact with more than thirty different people in the coming month, whether you are a parent, manager, coach, doctor, teacher, cleric, or in some other helping role. We are asking you to have just *one* fifteen- to twenty-minute conversation—within the 960 waking minutes available to each of us every day—focused on helping someone experience positive emotions and discover or reconnect with his or her personal vision. It could be over coffee, lunch, or driving in the company or school carpool. Or you could talk with a group at work about the idea, perhaps as an opener or closer to a staff meeting. Then imagine each of those people feeling so inspired that they in turn cascade the conversation to someone else they know, and so on. As a result of emotional contagion and social mimicry, the compounding effect could be tremendous. Large numbers of people will have had a potentially life-changing positive emotional experience based on being coached with compassion and thinking about their personal vision of the future. All this from one humble start: a fifteen- to twenty-minute coaching conversation!

We hope the stories and ideas in this book have inspired you to try a few things to ignite the spark of positive change in your life and the lives of people around you. Our deepest wish is that you will feel the hope, compassion, mindfulness, and playfulness that can result from caring for others and inspiring them to enhance their lives. That is the promise of coaching with compassion.

NOTES

CHAPTER 1

1. D. De La Cruz, "What Kids Wish Their Teachers Knew," *New York Times*, August 31, 2016; K. Schwartz, *I Wish My Teacher Knew: How One Question Can Change Everything for Our Kids* (Boston: Da Capo Lifelong Books, 2016).

2. De La Cruz, "What Kids Wish Their Teachers Knew."

CHAPTER 2

1. For more on the definition and evolution of coaching, see M. Smith, E. Van Oosten, and R. E. Boyatzis, "Coaching for Sustained Desired Change," in *Research in Organization Development and Change*, vol. 17, ed. R. W. Woodman, W. A. Pasmore, and A. B. Shani (Bingley, UK: Emerald Group Publishing, 2009), 145–174. Other articles on definitions of coaching include: V. V. Vandaveer et al., "A Practice Analysis of Coaching Psychology: Toward a Foundational Competency Model," *Consulting Psychology Journal: Practice and Research* 68 (2016): 118–142; R. R. Kilburg, "The Development of Human Expertise: Toward a Model for the 21st-Century Practice of Coaching, Consulting, and General Applied Psychology," *Consulting Psychology Journal: Practice and Research* 6 (2016): 177–187; R. R. Kilburg, "Toward a Conceptual Understanding and Definition of Executive Coaching," *Consulting Psychology Journal: Practice and Research* 48, no. 2 (1996): 134–144; D. B. Peterson, "Executive Coaching: A Critical Review and Recommendations for Advancing the Practice," in *APA Handbook of Industrial and Organizational Psychology*, vol. 2, *Selecting and Developing Members of the Organization* (Washington, DC: American Psychological Association, 2010), 527–566.

2. *ICF Definition of Coaching*, 2018; retrieved from https://coachfederation.org/about.

3. *Growth of professional coaching/surveys of coaching:* A. M. Liljenstrand and D. M. Nebeker, "Coaching Services: A Look at Coaches,

Clients and Practices," *Consulting Psychology Journal* 60, no. 1 (2008): 57–77; *ICF Global Coaching Study: Executive Summary*, International Coaching Federation, 2012; retrieved from http://www.coachfederation .org/coachingstudy2012; *2013 ICF Organizational Coaching Study*, 2013; retrieved from http://coachfederation.org/orgstudy; Sherpa Coaching, *The Tenth Annual Executive Coaching Survey* (Cincinnati, OH: Sherpa Coaching, 2015).

Coaching contexts: R. E. Boyatzis, M. L. Smith, and A. J. Beveridge, "Coaching with Compassion: Inspiring Health, Well-Being, and Development in Organizations,"*Journal of Applied Behavioral Science* 49, no. 2 (2013): 153–178.

4. Outcome studies of coaching itself—not including therapy, teaching, counseling, and other forms of helping—have shown positive impact on the coachees, in particular in their improvement of well-being, self-perceived change, and their relationship with the coach; see A. Athanasopoulou and S. Dopson, "A Systematic Review of Executive Coaching Outcomes: Is It the Journey or the Destination That Matters the Most?" *Leadership Quarterly*, 29, no. 1 (2018): 70–88; A. M. Grant, "What Can Sydney Tell Us about Coaching? Research with Implications for Practice from Down Under," *Consulting Psychology Journal: Practice and Research* 68 (2016): 105–117; E. de Haan et al., "A Large Scale Study of Executive and Workplace Coaching: The Relative Contributions of Relationship, Personality Match, and Self-Efficacy," *Consulting Psychology Journal: Practice and Research* 68, no. 3 (2016): 189 –207; T. Bachkirova and S. Borrington, "Old Wine in New Bottles: Exploring Pragmatism as a Philosophical Framework for the Discipline of Coaching," *Academy of Management Learning and Education* (2018); W. J. G. Evers, A. Brouwers, and W. Tomic, "A Quasi-Experimental Study on Management Coaching Effectiveness," *Consulting Psychology Journal: Practice and Research* 58 (2006): 174 –182; E. de Haan et al., "Executive Coaching Outcome Research: The Contribution of Common Factors Such as Relationship, Personality Match, and Self-Efficacy," *Consulting Psychology Journal: Practice and Research* 65 (2013): 40–57; A. M. Grant, *Workplace, Executive and Life Coaching: An Annotated Bibliography from the Behavioural Science and Business Literature* (Sydney, Australia: University of Sydney Coaching Psychology Unit, 2011); T. Theeboom, B. Beersma, and E. M. Van Wianen, "Does Coaching Work? A Meta-Analysis on the Effects of Coaching on Individual Level Outcomes in an Organizational Context," *Journal of Positive Psychology* 9, no. 1 (September 2013): 1–18; G. A. Sforzo et al., "Compendium of the Health and Wellness Coaching Literature," *Journal of Lifestyle Medicine* 12, no. 6 (2018); R. Jones, S. Woods, and Y. Guillaume,

"The Effectiveness of Workplace Coaching: A Meta-Analysis of Learning and Performance Outcomes from Coaching," *Journal of Occupational and Organizational Psychology* 89 (2015): 249–277.

5. Detailed results of these longitudinal coaching outcome studies can be found in: R. E. Boyatzis and K. V. Cavanagh, "Leading Change: Developing Emotional, Social, and Cognitive Competencies in Managers during an MBA Program," in *Emotional Intelligence in Education: Integrating Research into Practice*, ed. K. V. Keefer, J. D. A. Parker, and D. H. Saklofske (New York: Springer, 2018), 403–426; E. Amdurer et al., "Longitudinal Impact of Emotional, Social and Cognitive Intelligence Competencies on Career and Life Satisfaction and Career Success," *Frontiers in Psychology* 5, article 1447 (2014), doi:10.3389 /fpsyg.2014.01447; R. E. Boyatzis, A. Passarelli, and H. Wei, "Developing Emotional, Social, and Cognitive Competencies in MBA Programs: A Twenty-Five Year Perspective," in *Leader Interpersonal and Influence Skills: The Soft Skills of Leadership*, ed. R. Riggio and S. Tan (London: Routledge, 2013): 311–330; A. Passarelli, R. E. Boyatzis and H. Wei, "Assessing Leader Development: Lessons from a Historical Review of MBA Outcomes," *Journal of Management Education* 42, no. 1 (2018): 55–79; R. E. Boyatzis, A. Lingham, and A. Passarelli, "Inspiring the Development of Emotional, Social, and Cognitive Intelligence Competencies in Managers," in *Self-Management and Leadership Development*, ed. M. Rothstein and R. Burke (Cheltenham, UK: Edward Elgar Publishers, 2010), 62–90; R. E. Boyatzis and A. Saatcioglu, "A Twenty-Year View of Trying to Develop Emotional, Social and Cognitive Intelligence Competencies in Graduate Management Education," *Journal of Management Development* 27, no. 3 (2008): 92–108; R. E. Boyatzis, E. C. Stubbs, and S. N. Taylor, "Learning Cognitive and Emotional Intelligence Competencies through Graduate Management Education," *Academy of Management Journal on Learning and Education* 1, no. 2 (2002): 150–162; R. Ballou et al., "Fellowship in Lifelong Learning: An Executive Development Program for Advanced Professionals," *Journal of Management Education* 23, no. 4 (1999): 338–354; R. E. Boyatzis et al., "Competencies Can Be Developed but Not in the Way We Thought," *Capability* 2, no. 2 (1996): 25–41; R. E. Boyatzis, "Consequences and Rejuvenation of Competency-Based Human Resource and Organization Development," in *Research in Organizational Change and Development*, vol. 9, ed. R. W. Woodman and W. A. Pasmore (Greenwich, CT: JAI Press, 1996), 101–122; R. E. Boyatzis and A. Renio, "The Impact of an MBA Program on Managerial Abilities," *Journal of Management Development* 8, no. 5 (1989): 66–77; R. E. Boyatzis et al., "Will It Make a Difference?

Assessing a Value-Based, Outcome Oriented, Competency Based Professional Program," *Innovating in Professional Education: Steps on a Journey from Teaching to Learning* (San Francisco: Jossey-Bass, 1995), 167–202; L. Mosteo et al., "Understanding Cognitive-Emotional Processing through a Coaching Process: The Influence of Coaching on Vision, Goal-Directed Energy, and Resilience," *Journal of Applied Behavioral Science* 52, no. 1 (2016): 64–96; D. C. Leonard, "The Impact of Learning Goals on Emotional, Social, and Cognitive Intelligence Competency Development," *Journal of Management Development* 27, no. 1 (2008): 109–128; K. Rhee, "The Beat and Rhythm of Competency Development over Two Years," *Journal of Management Development* 12, no. 1 (2008): 146–160; J. V. Wheeler, "The Impact of Social Environments on Emotional, Social, and Cognitive Competency Development," *Journal of Management Development* 27, no. 1 (2008): 129–145.

6. For detailed study results, see R. E. Boyatzis, "Leadership Development from a Complexity Perspective," *Consulting Psychology Journal: Practice and Research* 60, no. 4 (2008): 298–313.

7. Some question the use of self-disclosure in coaching or in psychotherapy. Tatiana Bachkirova writes about the importance of "the self of the coach" ("The Self of the Coach: Conceptualization, Issues, and Opportunities for Practitioner Development," *Consulting Psychology Journal: Practice and Research* 68, no. 2 [2016]: 143–156). Many others over the years have written about the value of appropriately used self-disclosure to aid a coachee's development; see for instance S. M. Jourard, *Self-Disclosure: An Experimental Analysis of the Transparent Self* (Ann Arbor, MI: Wiley-Interscience, 1971).

8. For more on the psychological and behavioral level, read E. Hatfield, J. T. Cacioppo, and R. L. Rapson, *Emotional Contagion: Studies in Emotion and Social Interaction* (New York: Cambridge University Press, 1993); and more recently, the work of H. A. Elfenbein, "The Many Faces of Emotional Contagion: An Affective Process Theory of Affective Linkage," *Organizational Psychology Review* 4, no. 4, (2014): 326–362.

CHAPTER 3

1. See Ron Ashkenas, "Change Management Needs to Change," *Harvard Business Review*, April 2013.

2. M. T. Brown, MD, and J. K. Bussell, MD, "Medication Adherence: WHO Cares?" *Mayo Clinic Proceedings* 86, no. 4 (April 2011): 304–314.

3. Melvin's coach was Meg Seelbach from the Weatherhead Executive Education coaching pool.

4. Intentional Change Theory began in the late 1960s when Richard Boyatzis joined David Kolb, then a professor at MIT and later at Case Western Reserve University. In the early years, it was called *self-directed behavior change*. This resulted in a series of studies on helping and its impact (see D. A. Kolb and R. E. Boyatzis, "On the Dynamics of the Helping Relationship," *Journal of Applied Behavioral Science* 6, no. 3 [1970]: 267–290; and D. A. Kolb and R. E. Boyatzis, "Goal Setting and Self-Directed Behavior Change," *Human Relations* 23, no. 5 [1970]: 439–457). In the late 1990s, the theory emerged as ICT when it became clear that it was a fractal at many levels of sustained, desired change within human systems. The research had revealed significant discontinuities, so elements of nonlinear dynamics and complexity theory were used to explain the revised theory (see R. E. Boyatzis, "Intentional Change Theory from a Complexity Perspective," *Journal of Management Development* 25, no. 7 [2006]: 607–623); R. E. Boyatzis, "Coaching with Intentional Change Theory," in *The Professional Coach's Desk Reference*, ed. P. Brownell, S. English, and J. Sabatine [New York: Springer, 2017]).

5. R. E. Boyatzis and K. Akrivou, "The Ideal Self as the Driver of Intentional Change," *Journal of Management Development* 25, no. 7 (2006): 624–642.

6. Dewitt Jones, *Celebrate What's Right with the World* (video), Star Thrower Distributions, 2010.

7. S. N. Taylor, "Redefining Leader Self-Awareness by Integrating the Second Component of Self-Awareness," *Journal of Leadership Studies* 3, no. 4 (2010): 57–68; S. N. Taylor, "Student Self-Assessment and Multi-source Feedback Assessment: Exploring Benefits, Limitations, and Remedies," *Journal of Management Education* 38, no. 3 (2014): 359–383.

8. For an alternative approach, see M. Goldsmith, "Try Feedforward Instead of Feedback," *Leader to Leader* 25 (Summer 2002): 11–14.

9. M. Maltz, *Psycho-Cybernetics* (New York: Simon and Schuster, 1960).

10. S. Covey, *The Seven Habits of Highly Effective People* (New York: Simon and Schuster, 1989).

11. M. Gladwell, *Outliers: The Story of Success* (New York: Little, Brown and Company, 2008).

12. P. Lally et al., "How Are Habits Formed: Modelling Habit Formation in the Real World," *European Journal of Social Psychology* 40 (2010): 998–1009.

13. See D. Goleman, *Emotional Intelligence* (New York: Bantam Books, 1995); D. Goleman, *Working with Emotional Intelligence* (New York: Bantam Books, 1998); R. Boyatzis and D. Goleman, *Emotional and Social Competency Inventory* (2007), distributed worldwide by Korn Ferry; D. Goleman, R. E. Boyatzis, and A. McKee, *Primal Leadership: Realizing the Power of Emotional Intelligence* (Boston: Harvard Business School Press, 2002); R. E. Boyatzis, "The Behavioral Level of Emotional Intelligence and Its Measurement," *Frontiers in Psychology* 9, article 1438 (August 13, 2018), doi:10.3389/fpsyg.2018.01438; D. Goleman and R. E. Boyatzis, "Social Intelligence and the Biology of Leadership," *Harvard Business Review*, September, 2008, pp. 74–81.

14. D. Dunning, "On Identifying Human Capital: Flawed Knowledge Leads to Faulty Judgments of Expertise by Individuals and Groups," *Advances in Group Processes* 32 (2015): 149–176; see also D. Goleman, *Vital Lies, Simple Truths: The Psychology of Self-Deception* (New York: Simon and Schuster, 1985).

15. For studies evaluating coaching styles, see: E. de Haan and V. O. Nilsson, "Evaluating Coaching Behavior in Managers, Consultants, and Coaches: A Model, Questionnaire, and Initial Findings," *Consulting Psychology Journal: Practice and Research* 69, no. 4 (2017): 315; C. W. Coultas and E. Salas, "Identity Construction in Coaching: Schemas, Information Processing, and Goal Commitment," *Consulting Psychology Journal: Practice and Research* 67, no. 4 (2015): 298; R. T. Y. Hui and C. Sue Chan, "Variations in Coaching Style and Their Impact on Subordinates' Work Outcomes," *Journal of Organizational Behavior* 39, no 5 (2018): 663–679; C. Kauffman and W. H. Hodgetts, "Model Agility: Coaching Effectiveness and Four Perspectives on a Case Study," *Consulting Psychology Journal: Practice and Research* 68 (2016): 157–176; G. Bozer and B-K. Joo, "The Effects of Coachee Characteristics and Coaching Relationships on Feedback Receptivity and Self-Awareness in Executive Coaching," *International Leadership Journal* 7, no. 3 (2015): 36–58; G. Bozer, B-K. Joo, and J. C. Santora, "Executive Coaching: Does Coach-Coachee Matching Based on Similarity Really Matter?" *Consulting Psychology Journal: Practice and Research* 67, no. 3 (2015): 218–233.

16. Kauffman and Hodgetts, "Model Agility."

17. See studies referenced in Goleman, Boyatzis, and McKee, *Primal Leadership*, 105–108.

18. R. E. Boyatzis et al., "Coaching Can Work, but Doesn't Always," *People Management*, March 11, 2004.

CHAPTER 4

1. The shift in focus in educational settings is so profound that although John Dewey wrote about it in the 1920s (J. Dewey, *Experience and Education*, Kappa Delta Pi [1938]), learner-centered development has often been viewed as an experiment done by people who "smoked too much" (an erroneous and disparaging allusion to the likelihood that they were using mind-altering substances without medicinal need). For decades, the Montessori Method was seen by many as catering to and pampering children when instead, the Montessori teachers were trying to use the natural curiosity and energy of each child to aid in their learning.

2. *Outcome assessment early works*: R. Albanese et al., "Outcome Measurement and Management Education: An Academy of Management Task Force Report" (presentation at the Annual Academy of Management Meeting, San Francisco, 1990); A. W. Astin, *What Matters in College? Four Critical Years* (San Francisco: Jossey-Bass, 1993); T. W. Banta, ed., *Making a Difference: Outcomes of a Decade of Assessment in Higher Education* (San Francisco: Jossey-Bass, 1993); M. Mentkowski et. al, "Understanding Abilities, Learning and Development through College Outcome Studies: What Can We Expect from Higher Education Assessment?" (paper presented at the Annual Meeting of the American Educational Research Association, Chicago, 1991); M. Mentkowski and Associates, *Learning That Lasts: Integrating Learning, Development, and Performance in College and Beyond* (San Francisco: Jossey-Bass, 2000); E. T. Pascarella and P. T. Terenzini, *How College Affects Students: Findings and Insights from Twenty Years of Research* (San Francisco: Jossey-Bass, 1991).

Learning as output in education: In education, learning is the output. But because education has been framed most often as an expert system, with the teachers (and administrators) knowing more about the process than the students or parents, the focus is more often on what someone is teaching than on what the students are learning.

Outcome assessment in higher education began in earnest in the early 1970s to help colleges and universities experiment and adjust their processes to what was called "nontraditional students" at the time (see references on outcome assessment early works, above). That was the label being used for college students who were over twenty-one, female, or members of visible minority groups. President George H. Bush passed an executive order in 1989 requiring that any accrediting body that sought federal funding would have to require colleges and programs to use outcome assessment to show what it was that their students were actually learning. Earlier that decade, the American Association of Collegiate Schools of Business (AACSB, which later changed its name to the Association of Academic and Collegiate Schools of Business), the group that accredits all business programs, began to explore whether reaccreditation and initial accreditation should be based on the stated purpose of a particular institution rather than on the number of books in their library, the number of faculty with PhDs, and such. These latter and at that time main criteria were called *input* characteristics. They were input to the development process. Questions about evidence as to what students were learning were called an *output* orientation.

This was a profound shift in focus that called for faculty and administrators to think more about the student than the faculty. It was not enough to say what faculty members claimed they were covering in their syllabus—you had to ask what the students were learning and then retaining weeks during the months after the course. This was asking the right question by placing the focus on the students.

3. Self-control is an emotional intelligence competency as described by D. Goleman, R. E. Boyatzis, and A. McKee in *Primal Leadership: Realizing the Power of Emotional Intelligence* (Boston: Harvard Business School Press, 2002). Numerous research studies show it is significantly predictive of effectiveness in helping; see R. E. Boyatzis, "Core Competencies in Coaching Others to Overcome Dysfunctional Behavior," in *Emotional Intelligence and Work Performance*, ed. V. Druskat, G. Mount, and F. Sala (Mahwah, NJ: Erlbaum, 2005), 81–95; and R. E. Boyatzis, "Emotional Intelligence," in *Sage Encyclopedia of Educational Research, Measurement, and Evaluation*, ed. Bruce Frey (Thousand Oaks, CA: Sage Publications, 2018), 579–580.

4. Edgar H. Schein, *Helping: How to Offer, Give, and Receive Help* (San Francisco: Berrett-Koehler, 2009).

5. D. De La Cruz, "What Kids Wish Their Teachers Knew," *New York Times*, August 31, 2016; K. Schwartz, *I Wish My Teacher Knew: How One Question Can Change Everything for Our Kids* (Boston: Da Capo Lifelong Books, 2016).

6. D. Goleman, *Focus: The Hidden Driver of Excellence* (New York: Harper Books, 2015).

7. R. E. Boyatzis, K. Rochford, and K. Cavanagh, "The Role of Emotional and Social Intelligence Competencies in Engineer's Effectiveness and Engagement," *Career Development International* 22, no. 1 (2017): 70–86.

8. During helping, trying to empathize can arouse threat (NEA) in the helper. Imagining the other person's feelings (i.e., putting yourself in his or her shoes) hurts the helper. A. E. K. Buffone et al., "Don't Walk

in Her Shoes! Different Forms of Perspective Taking Effect Stress Physiology," *Journal of Experimental Social Psychology* 72 (September 2017): 161–168.

9. A 360-degree assessment collects information from your boss, peers, subordinates, and possibly clients or even spouse or partner. For more understanding about the approach and the specific test, the ESCI (Emotional and Social Competency Inventory), see R. E. Boyatzis, "The Behavioral Level of Emotional Intelligence and Its Measurement," *Frontiers in Psychology* 9, article 1438 (2018): doi.org/10.3389 /fpsyg.2018.01438; J. M. Batista-Foguet et al., "Why Multisource Assessment and Feedback Has Been Erroneously Analyzed and How It Should Be," *Frontiers in Psychology* 9, article 2646 (2019): https://doi .org/10.3389/fpsyg.2018.02646; R. E. Boyatzis, "Commentary of Ackley (2016): Updates on the ESCI as the Behavioral Level of Emotional Intelligence," *Consulting Psychology Journal: Practice and Research* 68, no. 4 (2017): 287–293; R. E. Boyatzis, J. Gaskin, and H. Wei, "Emotional and Social Intelligence and Behavior," in *Handbook of Intelligence: Evolutionary, Theory, Historical Perspective, and Current Concepts*, ed. D. Princiotta, S. Goldstein, and J. Naglieri (New York: Spring Press, 2014), 243–262. For more information about using the ESCI, contact http://www.haygroup.com/leadershipandtalentondemand/ourproducts /item_details.aspx?itemid=58&type=2; Priscilla De San Juan Olle (Priscilla.Olle@KornFerry.com, at 617-927-5018).

10. R. F. Baumeister et al., "Bad Is Stronger Than Good," *Review of General Psychology* 5, no. 4 (2001): 323–370.

11. M. Khawaja, "The Mediating Role of Positive and Negative Emotional Attractors between Psychosocial Correlates of Doctor-Patient Relationship and Treatment of Type II Diabetes" (doctoral dissertation, Case Western Reserve University, 2011).

12. J. Groopman, *The Anatomy of Hope* (New York: Random House, 2000); Atul Gawande, *Being Mortal* (London: Picador, 2016).

13. We have two fMRI studies of PEA versus NEA coaching that show the neural mechanisms involved: A. I. Jack et al., "Visioning in the Brain: An fMRI Study of Inspirational Coaching and Mentoring," *Social Neuroscience* 8, no. 4 (2013): 369–384 (reviewed in A. Passarelli, "The Neuro-Emotional Basis of Developing Leaders through Personal Vision," *Frontiers in Psychology* 6, article 1335 [2015]: doi:10.3389/ fpsyg.2014.01335); and A. Passarelli et al., "Neuroimaging Reveals Link Between Vision and Coaching for Intentional Change," (in review) (also presented at the Annual Meeting of the Academy of Management, Vancouver, British Columbia, Canada, 2015).

14. The single best summary of research on stress is by R. Sapolsky, *Why Zebras Don't Get Ulcers*, 3rd ed. (New York: Harper Collins, 2004); other relevant reviews and discussions are found in S. C. Segerstrom and G. E. Miller, "Psychological Stress and the Human Immune System: A Meta-Analytic Study of 30 Years of Inquiry," *Psychological Bulletin* 130, no. 4 (2004): 601–630; S. S Dickerson and M. E. Kemeny, "Acute Stressors and Cortisol Responses: A Theoretical Integration and Synthesis of Laboratory Research," *Psychological Bulletin* 130 (2004): 355–391; R. E. Boyatzis, M. L. Smith, and N. Blaize, "Sustaining Leadership Effectiveness through Coaching and Compassion: It's Not What You Think," *Academy of Management Learning and Education* 5 (2006): 8–24.

15. E. Friedmann et al., "Animal Companions and One-Year Survival of Patients after Discharge from a Coronary Care Unit," *Public Health Reports* 95, no. 4 (1980): 307; and J. P. Polheber and R. L. Matchock, "The Presence of a Dog Attenuates Cortisol and Heart Rate in the Trier Social Stress Test Compared to Human Friends,"*Journal of Behavioral Medicine* 37, no. 5 (2014): 860–867.

16. R. Boyatzis and A. McKee, *Resonant Leadership: Renewing Yourself and Connecting with Others through Mindfulness, Hope, and Compassion* (Boston: Harvard Business School Press, 2005).

17. J. LeDoux, *The Emotional Brain: The Mysterious Underpinnings of Emotional Life* (New York: Touchstone Books, Simon & Shuster, 1996); J. LeDoux, *Synaptic Self: How Our Brains Become Who We Are* (New York: Viking, 2002).

18. B. Libet et al., "Subjective Referral of the Timing for a Conscious Sensory Experience," *Brain* 102, no. 1 (1979): 193–224.

19. *American Psychologist* 58, no. 1 (2003) is a collection of articles on religiosity and spirituality, their measurement and health benefits.

20. *Managerial humor and effectiveness:* F. Sala, "Relationship between Executives' Spontaneous Use of Humor and Effective Leadership" (unpublished PhD thesis, Boston University, 1996); F. Sala, "Laughing All the Way to the Bank," *Harvard Business Review* (September 2003).

Healing effects of humor: C. M. Greene et al., "Evaluation of a Laughter-Based Exercise Program on Health and Self-efficacy for Exercise," *The Gerontologist* 57, no. 6 (2016): 1051–1061; J. H. Han, K. M Park, and H. Park, "Effects of Laughter Therapy on Depression and Sleep among Patients at Long-Term Care Hospitals," *Korean Journal of Adult Nursing* 29, no. 5 (2017): 560–568; H. Ko and C. Youn, "Effects of Laughter Therapy on Depression, Cognition and Sleep among the Community-Dwelling Elderly," *Geriatrics and Gerontology International* 11 (2011): 267–274.

21. G. N. Bratman et al., "Nature Experience Reduces Rumination and Subgenual Prefrontal Cortex Activation," *Proceedings of the National Academy of Sciences*, 112, no. 28 (2015): 8567–8572; and G. N. Bratman et al., "The Benefits of Nature Experience: Improved Affect and Cognition," *Landscape and Urban Planning* 138 (2015): 41–50.

22. K. C. Rochford, "Relational Climate in the Work Place: Dimensions, Measurement and Validation" (unpublished qualifying paper, Case Western Reserve University, 2016); K. C. Rochford, "Intentionality in Workplace Relationships: The Role of Relational Self-Efficacy (unpublished doctoral dissertation, Case Western Reserve University, 2016); R. E. Boyatzis, "Measuring the Impact of Quality of Relationships through the Positive Emotional Attractor," in *Positive Psychology of Relationships*, ed. S. Donaldson and M. Rao (Santa Barbara, CA: Praeger Publishers, 2018), 193–209; R. E. Boyatzis, K. Rochford, and S. N. Taylor, "The Role of the Positive Emotional Attractor as Vision and Shared Vision: Toward Effective Leadership, Relationships and Engagement," *Frontiers in Psychology* 6, article 670 (May 21, 2015), http://dx.doi.org/10.3389/fpsyg.2015.00670.

CHAPTER 5

1. Our apologies to any snake lovers or those with snakes as pets. We are not disparaging them but merely pointing out that we know of no scientific evidence to suggest that snakes seek novelty or affective pleasure. Meanwhile, there is evidence of all of those states for mammals from elephants to dogs and cats to dolphins, and primates from chimpanzees to humans.

2. R. E. Boyatzis, M. Smith, and N. Blaize, "Developing Sustainable Leaders through Coaching and Compassion," *Academy of Management Journal on Learning and Education* 5, no. 1 (2006): 8–24; R. E. Boyatzis, M. L. Smith, and A. J. Beveridge, "Coaching with Compassion: Inspiring Health, Well-Being, and Development in Organizations," *Journal of Applied Behavioral Science* 49, no. 2 (2012): 153–178.

3. R. E. Boyatzis, "When Pulling to the Negative Emotional Attractor Is Too Much or Not Enough to Inspire and Sustain Outstanding Leadership," in *The Fulfilling Workplace: The Organization's Role in Achieving Individual and Organizational Health*, ed. R. Burke, C. Cooper, and G. Woods (London: Gower Publishing, 2013), 139–150.

4. The preliminary stories from these cases were presented at the Institute of Coaching annual meeting in Boston in 2012 and in R. E. Boyatzis et al., "Developing Resonant Leaders through Emotional Intelligence, Vision and Coaching," *Organizational Dynamics* 42 (2013): 17–24.

5. Renewal is supported when a person is internally consistent and congruent. It is a state of being mindful, which we have discussed previously and in depth in previous articles and books. In R. E. Boyatzis and A. McKee, *Resonant Leadership: Renewing Yourself and Connecting with Others through Mindfulness, Hope, and Compassion* (Boston: Harvard Business School Press, 2005) and A. McKee, R. E. Boyatzis, and F. Johnston, *Becoming a Resonant Leader* (Boston: Harvard Business School Press, 2008), we claimed that the integration and congruence is within a person's mind, body, physical health and spiritual health. For that reason, these are all dimensions we typically ask someone to consider in developing his or her personal vision. When acting holistically, all aspects of the person can work toward the same sense of purpose. When one of these works in a different manner than the others, energy and attention is diverted from, if not in conflict with, the other aspects of the person. Humans seem to act most effectively and efficiently when all are in synchrony. For more details, see Boyatzis, Smith, and Blaize, "Developing Sustainable Leaders"; and Boyatzis and McKee, *Resonant Leadership*.

6. R. F. Baumeister, "The Nature and Structure of the Self: An Overview," in *The Self in Social Psychology*, ed. R. F. Baumeister (Philadelphia: Psychology Press, 1999), 1–20; R. F. Baumeister et al., "Bad Is Stronger Than Good,"*Review of General Psychology* 5, no. 4 (2001): 323–370.

7. A. Howard, "Coaching to Vision Versus Coaching to Improvement Needs: A Preliminary Investigation on the Differential Impacts of Fostering Positive and Negative Emotion during Real-Time Executive Coaching Sessions," *Frontiers in Psychology* 6, article 455 (2015): https://doi.org/10.3389/fpsyg.2015.00455; and R. E. Boyatzis and A. Howard, "When Goal Setting Helps and Hinders Sustained, Desired Change," in *Goal Setting and Goal Management in Coaching and Mentoring*, ed. S. David, D. Clutterbuck, and D. Megginson (Abington, UK: Taylor and Francis, 2013), 211–228.

8. A. I. Jack et al., "fMRI Reveals Reciprocal Inhibition between Social and Physical Cognitive Domains," *NeuroImage*, 66C (2012): 385–401; A. I. Jack, A. J. Dawson, and M. Norr, "Seeing Human: Distinct and Overlapping Neural Signatures Associated with Two Forms of Dehumanization," *NeuroImage* 79, no. 1 (2013): 313–328; A. I. Jack et al., "Why Do You Believe in God? Relationships between Religious Belief, Analytic Thinking, Mentalizing and Moral Concern," *PLOSONE* (2016); M. E. Raichle, "Two Views of Brain Function" *Trends in Cognitive Sciences* 14 (2010): 180–190; F. Van Overwalle,

"A Dissociation between Social Mentalizing and General Reasoning," *NeuroImage* 54 (2010): 1589–1599; M. D. Fox et al., "The Human Brain Is Intrinsically Organized into Dynamic, Anti-Correlated Functional Networks," *Proceedings of the National Academy of Sciences of the USA* 102, no. 27 (2005): 9673–9678; R. L. Buckner, J. R. Andrews-Hanna, and D. L. Schacter, "The Brain's Default Network," *Annals of the New York Academy of Sciences* 1124, no. 1 (2008): 1–38. Anthony Jack is concerned about using the historic names for these networks, because they are misleading. For example, the *default mode network* was originally used to suggest we use this network more at rest than when we are engaged in any kind of task. This network is far more active than at rest when people intentionally use empathy to understsand others. The label *task positive network* is also misleading, he says. This network is actually suppressed when people intentionaly engage in empathic tasks. The *analytic network* label is more strongly associated with action-oriented processing.

9. For a more detailed discussion within the context of coaching, see R. E. Boyatzis and A. I. Jack, "The Neuroscience of Coaching," *Consulting Psychology Journal* 70, no. 1 (2018): 11–27.

10. R. Boyatzis, A. McKee, and D. Goleman, "Reawakening Your Passion for Work," *Harvard Business Review*, April 2002, 86–94.

11. For more detail on recent neuroscience research and its relevance to coaching, see Boyatzis and Jack, "The Neuroscience of Coaching."

12. J. E. Zull, *The Art of Changing the Brain: Enriching Teaching by Exploring the Biology of Learning* (Sterling, VA: Stylus, 2002).

13. Several thousand studies about ELT are reviewed in D. A. Kolb, *Experiential Learning Theory* (Englewood Cliffs, NJ: Prentice Hall, 2015).

14. For those interested in how the two networks can contribute to ethical leadership, a detailed discussion can be found in K. Rochford et al., "Neural Roots of Ethical Leadership and the Development of Better Leaders: The Default Mode Network versus the Task Positive Network," *Journal of Business Ethics* 144, no. 4 (2016): 755–770.

15. The first of these studies was published by A. I. Jack et al. ("Visioning in the Brain: An fMRI Study of Inspirational Coaching and Mentoring," *Social Neuroscience* 8, no. 4 [2013]: 369–384); and reviewed in A. Passarelli ("Vision-Based Coaching: Optimizing Resources for Leader Development," *Frontiers in Psychology* 6 [2015], https://doi.org/10.3389/fpsyg.2015.00412); also see A. Passarelli et al., "Neuroimaging Reveals Link between Vision and Coaching for Intentional

Change" (in review); also presented at the Annual Meeting of the Academy of Management, Vancouver, British Columbia, August 8, 2015.

16. C. Camerer and D. Lovallo, "Overconfidence and Excess Entry: An Experimental Approach," *American Economic Review* 89, no. 1 (1999): 306–318.

17. Jack, Dawson, and Norr, "Seeing Human"; Rochford et al., "Neural Roots of Ethical Leadership."

18. S. S. Dickerson and M. E. Kemeny, "Acute Stressors and Cortisol Responses: A Theoretical Integration and Synthesis of Laboratory Research," *Psychological Bulletin* 130, no. 3 (2004): 355–391; B. S. McEwen, "Protective and Damaging Effects of Stress Mediators," *New England Journal of Medicine* 338 (1998): 171–179; R. M. Sapolsky, *Why Zebras Don't Get Ulcers*, 3rd ed. (New York: Harper Collins, 2004); S. C. Segerstom and G. E. Miller, "Psychological Stress and the Human Immune System: A Meta-Analytic Study of 30 Years of Inquiry," *Psychological Bulletin* 130, no. 4 (2004): 601–630; F. G. Asby, A. M. Isen, and A. U. Turken, "A Neuropsychological Theory of Positive Affect and Its Influence on Cognition," *Psychological Review* 106, no. 3 (1999): 529–550.

19. Dickerson and Kemeny, "Acute Stressors and Cortisol Responses"; McEwen, Protective and Damaging Effects of Stress Mediators"; Sapolsky, *Why Zebras Don't Get Ulcers*; Segerstom and Miller, "Psychological Stress and the Human Immune System"; Asby, Isen, and Turken, "A Neuropsychological Theory of Positive Affect."

20. Baumeister, "The Nature and Structure of the Self"; Baumeister et al., "Bad Is Stronger Than Good."

21. Often erroneously attributed to Aristotle, Plato, or Socrates, "nothing in excess" really comes from Kleovoulos (Diogenes Laërtius, "Cleobulus," *Lives of the Eminent Philosophers*, vol. 1, trans R. D. Hicks [Cambridge, MA: Loeb Classical Library, 1925], chapter 6.

22. B. L. Fredrickson, "The Role of Positive Emotions in Positive Psychology: The Broaden-and-Build Theory of Positive Emotions," *American Psychologist* 56, no. 3 (2001): 218–226; B. L. Fredrickson, "The Broaden-and-Build Theory of Positive Emotions," *Philosophical Transactions of the Royal Society of London B: Biological Sciences* 359, no. 1449 (2004): 1367–1378; B. L. Fredrickson, "Updated Thinking on Positivity Ratios," *American Psychologist* 68, no. 9 (2013): 814–822.

23. J. M. Gottman et al., *The Mathematics of Marriage: Dynamic Non-Linear Models* (Cambridge, MA: MIT Press, 2002).

24. fMRI studies of PEA versus NEA coaching are reviewed in Boyatzis and Jack, "The Neuroscience of Coaching"; and Jack et al.,

"Visioning in the Brain"; and reviewed in Passarelli, "The Neuro-Emotional Basis of Developing Leaders"; Passarelli et al., "Neuroimaging Reveals Link."

25. N. I. Eisenberger and S. W. Cole, "Social Neuroscience and Health: Neurophysiological Mechanisms Linking Social Ties with Physical Health," *Nature Neuroscience* 15, no. 5 (2012): 669–674; N. I. Eisenberger and M. D. Lieberman, "Why Rejection Hurts: A Common Neural Alarm System for Physical and Social Pain," *Trends in Cognitive Science* 8, no. 7 (2004): 294–300.

26. R. E. Boyatzis, K. Rochford, and S. N. Taylor, "The Role of the Positive Emotional Attractor in Vision and Shared Vision: Toward Effective Leadership, Relationships, and Engagement," *Frontiers in Psychology* 6, article 670 (2015), doi:10.3389/fpsyg.2015.00670; Fredrickson, "The Role of Positive Emotions"; Gottman et al., *The Mathematics of Marriage.*

27. L. Mosteo et al., "Understanding Cognitive-Emotional Processing through a Coaching Process: The Influence of Coaching on Vision, Goal-Directed Energy, and Resilience," *Journal of Applied Behavioral Science* 52, no. 1 (2016): 64–96.

28. The assessment of the amount of time a person spends in stress versus in renewal during a week and the variety of stress and renewal activities are assessed in Boyatzis and Goleman's Personal Sustainability Index (forthcoming). Read more about it and take the assessment in R. E. Boyatzis et al., "Thrive and Survive: Validation of the Personal Sustainability Index" (in review).

29. D. C. McClelland et al., *The Drinking Man: Alcohol and Human Motivation* (New York: Free Press, 1972); R. E. Boyatzis, "Power Motivation Training: A New Treatment Modality," in *Work in Progress on Alcoholism: Annals of the New York Academy of Sciences,* ed. F. Seixas and S. Eggleston (New York: Academy of Sciences, 1976), 273; H. Cutter, R. E. Boyatzis, and D. Clancy, "The Effectiveness of Power Motivation Training for Rehabilitating Alcoholics," *Journal of Studies on Alcohol* 38, no. 1 (1977): 131–141.

30. Personal Sustainability Index; Boyatzis et al., "Thrive and Survive."

31. Boyatzis et al., "Thrive and Survive."

CHAPTER 6

1. Diana Nyad interview with Sanjay Gupta, *CNN with Anderson Cooper,* September 2, 2013.

2. See R. Boyatzis and A. McKee, *Resonant Leadership: Renewing Yourself and Connecting with Others through Mindfulness, Hope, and Compassion* (Boston: Harvard Business School Press, 2005),

chapters 4–5; and also discussed in D. Goleman, R. E. Boyatzis, and A. McKee, *Primal Leadership: Realizing the Power of Emotional Intelligence* (Boston: Harvard Business School Press, 2002).

3. For discussion of the components of a personal vision, see R. E. Boyatzis and K. Akrivou, "The Ideal Self as the Driver of Intentional Change," *Journal of Management Development* 25, no. 7 (2006): 624–642; E. T. Higgins, "Self-Discrepancy: A Theory Relating Self and Affect,"*Psychological Review* 94, no. 3 (1987): 319–340.

4. L. Carroll, *Alice's Adventures in Wonderland* (New York: Puffin Books, 2015), 80. Originally published in 1865.

5. See A. M. Passarelli, "Vision-Based Coaching: Optimizing Resources for Leader Development," *Frontiers in Psychology* 6, article 412 (2015), doi:10.3389/fpsyg.2015.00412; and the more complete study A. M. Passarelli, "The Heart of Helping: Psychological and Physiological Effects of Contrasting Coaching Interactions" (unpublished doctoral dissertation, Case Western Reserve University, 2014).

6. R. Boyatzis and D. Goleman, *Emotional and Social Competency Inventory* (Boston: The Hay Group, 2007).

7. R. E. Boyatzis and U. Dhar, "The Evolving Ideal Self," unpublished paper, Case Western Reserve University, Cleveland, OH, 2019; and R. Kegan, *The Evolving Self: Problem and Process in Human Development* (Cambridge, MA: Harvard University Press, 1982).

8. R. E. Boyatzis and D. A. Kolb, "Performance, Learning, and Development as Modes of Growth and Adaptation throughout Our Lives and Careers," in *Career Frontiers: New Conceptions of Working Lives*, ed. M. Peiperl et al. (London: Oxford University Press, 1999), 76–98.

9. High need for achievement is one of the motivations defined in D. C. McClelland, *Human Motivation* (Glenview, IL: Scott Foresman and Co., 1985).

10. J. F. Brett and D. Vandewalle, "Goal Orientation and Goal Content as Predictors of Performance in a Training Program," *Journal of Applied Psychology* 84, no. 6 (1999): 863–887; D. A. Kolb and R. E. Boyatzis, "Goal-Setting and Self-Directed Behavior Change," *Human Relations* 23, no. 5 (1970): 439–457; E. A. Locke and G. P. Latham, *A Theory of Goal Setting and Task Performance* (Englewood Cliffs, NJ: Prentice-Hall, 1990); D. Vandewalle et al., "The Influence of Goal Orientation and Self-Regulation Tactics on Sales Performance: A Longitudinal Field Test," *Journal of Applied Psychology* 84, no. 2 (1999): 249–259.

11. G. H. Seijts et al., "Goal Setting and Goal Orientation: An Integration of Two Different Yet Related Literatures," *Academy of Management Journal* 47, no. 2 (2004): 227–239; R. E. Boyatzis and A. Howard, "When Goal Setting Helps and Hinders Sustained, Desired Change," in *Goal Setting and Goal Management in Coaching and Mentoring*, ed. S. David, D. Clutterbuck, and D. Megginson (New York: Routledge, 2013), 211–228.

12. W. W. Seeley et al., "Dissociable Intrinsic Connectivity Networks for Salience Processing and Executive Control," *Journal of Neuroscience* 27 (2007): 2349–2356; D. Ming et al., "Examining Brain Structures Associated with the Motive to Achieve Success and the Motive to Avoid Failure: A Voxel-Based Morphometry Study," *Social Neuroscience* 11, no. 1 (2007): 38–48; more recent research suggests that internal goal-directed thought, as with autobiography and even vision and purpose development, will activate parts of the EN; see A. Elton and W. Gao, "Task-Positive Functional Connectivity of the Default Mode Network Transcends Task Domain," *Journal of Cognitive Neuroscience* 27, no. 12 (2015): 2369–2381.

13. E. T. Higgins, "Self-Discrepancy: A Theory Relating Self and Affect,"*Psychological Review* 94, no. 3 (1987): 319–340; J. Brockner and E. T. Higgins, "Regulatory Focus Theory: Implications for the Study of Emotions at Work," *Annual Review of Psychology* 86, no. 1 (2001): 35–66.

14. A. Passarelli et al., "Neuroimaging Reveals Link between Vision and Coaching for Intentional Change" (in review) (also presented at the Academy of Management, Philadelphia, August 14, 2014); A. Howard, "Coaching to Vision versus Coaching to Improvement Needs: A Preliminary Investigation on the Differential Impacts of Fostering Positive and Negative Emotion during Real Time Executive Coaching Sessions," *Frontiers in Psychology* 6, article 455 (2015), doi:10.3389/fpsyg.2015.00455; Passarelli, "Vision-Based Coaching"; R. E. Boyatzis, and A. Jack, "The Neuroscience of Coaching," *Consulting Psychology Journal* 70, no. 1 (2018): 11–27; A. Passarelli et al., "Seeing the Big Picture: fMRI Reveals Neural Overlap between Coaching and Visual Attention" (in review); A. Jack et al., "Visioning in the Brain: An fMRI Study of Inspirational Coaching and Mentoring," *Social Neuroscience* 8, no. 4 (2013): 369–384.

15. The studies mentioned earlier in the book were: Jack et al., "Visioning in the Brain"; Passarelli et al., "Neuroimaging Reveals Link."

16. Boyatzis and Akrivou, "The Ideal Self."

17. For the most comprehensive research on hope, see C. R. Snyder et al., "Development and Validation of the State Hope Model," *Journal of Personality and Social Psychology* 70 (1996): 321–335.

18. K. Buse and D. Bilimoria, "Personal Vision: Enhancing Work Engagement and the Retention of Women in the Engineering Profession," *Frontiers in Psychology* 5, article 1400 (2014). doi.org/10.3389 /fpsyg.2014.01400.

CHAPTER 7

1. Sean Hannigan was a participant in a leadership development program that the organization completed with CWRU, and he received 360-degree feedback on his emotional and social intelligence. This form of feedback, also known as multi-rater feedback, is commonly used in leadership development and coaching engagements. It invites raters who interact with the individual to answer survey questions and provide verbatim comments on their experience with the person. The raters may include a manager(s), direct reports, peers, clients, and customers.

2. J. Dutton and E. Heaphy, "The Power of High-Quality Connections," in *Positive Organizational Scholarship: Foundations of a New Discipline*, ed. K. S. Cameron, J. E. Dutton, and R. E. Quinn (San Francisco: Berrett-Koehler, 2003), 263–278; J. P. Stephens, E. Heaphy, and J. Dutton, "High-Quality Connections," in *The Oxford Handbook of Positive Organizational Scholarship*, ed. K. Cameron and G. Spreitzer (New York: Oxford University Press, 2011), 385–399.

3. Dutton and Heaphy, "The Power of High-Quality Connections."

4. J. P. Stephens et al., "Relationship Quality and Virtuousness: Emotional Carrying Capacity as a Source of Individual and Team Resilience," *Journal of Applied Behavioral Science* 49, no. 1 (2013): 13–41.

5. W. Murphy and K. Kram, *Strategic Relationships at Work* (New York: McGraw-Hill, 2014).

6. R. Boyatzis, "Intentional Change Theory from a Complexity Perspective," *Journal of Management Development* 25, no. 7 (2006): 607–623.

7. See R. E. Boyatzis, "Measuring the Impact of Quality of Relationships through the Positive Emotional Attractor," in *Toward a Positive Psychology of Relationships: New Directions in Theory and Research*, ed. M. Warren and S. Donaldson (Santa Barbara, CA: Praeger Publishers, 2018), 193–209; E. Hatfield, J. T. Cacioppo, and R. L. Rapson, *Emotional Contagion: Studies in Emotion and Social Interaction* (New York: Cambridge University Press,

1993); J. K. Hazy and R. E. Boyatzis, "Emotional Contagion and Proto-organizing in Human Dynamics," *Frontiers in Psychology* 6, article 806 (June 12, 2015), http://dx.doi.org/10.3389/fpsyg.2015.00806; R. E. Boyatzis, K. Rochford, and S. N. Taylor, "The Role of the Positive Emotional Attractor as Vision and Shared Vision: Toward Effective Leadership, Relationships and Engagement," *Frontiers in Psychology* 6, article 670 (May 21, 2015), http://dx.doi.org/10.3389/fpsyg.2015.00670; H. A. Elfenbein, "The Many Faces of Emotional Contagion: An Affective Process Theory of Affective Linkage," *Organizational Psychology Review* 4, no. 4 (August 8, 2014): 336–392; N. A. Christakis and J. H. Fowler, *Connected: The Surprising Power of Our Social Networks and How They Shape Our Lives—How Your Friends' Friends' Friends Affect Everything You Feel, Think, and Do* (Boston: Little, Brown and Spark, 2011).

8. Boyatzis, "Measuring the Impact of Quality of Relationships," ed. M. Warren and S. Donaldson.

9. R. E. Boyatzis and K. Rochford, *Relational Climate Survey* (2015); available from the authors at Case Western Reserve University.

10. M. Khawaja, "The Mediating Role of Positive and Negative Emotional Attractors between Psychosocial Correlates of Doctor-Patient Relationship and Treatment of Type II Diabetes" (doctoral dissertation, Case Western Reserve University, 2011).

11. E. Van Oosten, M. McBride-Walker, and S. Taylor, "Investing in What Matters: The Impact of Emotional and Social Competency Development and Executive Coaching on Leader Outcomes," *Consulting Psychology Journal* (in press); E. Van Oosten, "The Impact of Emotional Intelligence and Executive Coaching on Leader Effectiveness" (unpublished doctoral dissertation, Case Western Reserve University, 2013).

12. L. M. Pittenger, "Emotional and Social Competencies and Perceptions of the Interpersonal Environment of an Organization as Related to the Engagement of IT Professionals," *Frontiers in Psychology* 6, article 623 (2015), https://doi.org/10.3389/fpsyg.2015.00623.

13. M. Babu, "Characteristics of Effectiveness Leadership among Community College Presidents" (unpublished doctoral dissertation, Case Western Reserve University, 2016).

14. J. F. Quinn, "The Effect of Vision and Compassion upon Role Factors in Physician Leadership," *Frontiers in Psychology* 6, article 442 (2015), https://doi.org/10.3389/fpsyg.2015.00442.

15. L. Kendall, "A Theory of Micro-Level Dynamic Capabilities: How Technology Leaders Innovate with Human Connection" (unpublished doctoral dissertation, Case Western Reserve University, 2016).

16. J. E. Neff, "Shared Vision and Family Firm Performance," *Frontiers in Psychology* 6, article 646 (2015), https://doi.org/10.3389/fpsyg.2015.00646; S. P. Miller, "Next-Generation Leadership Development in Family Businesses: The Critical Roles of Shared Vision and Family Climate," *Frontiers in Psychology* 6, article 1335 (2015), doi:10.3389/fpsyg.2014.01335; S. P. Miller, "Developing Next Generation Leadership Talent in Family Businesses: The Family Effect" (unpublished doctoral dissertation, Case Western Reserve University, 2014).

17. K. Overbeke, D. Bilimoria, and T. Somers, "Shared Vision between Fathers and Daughters in Family Businesses: The Determining Factor That Transforms Daughters into Successors," *Frontiers in Psychology* 6, article 625 (2015), https://doi.org/10.3389/fpsyg.2015.00625.

18. E. G. Mahon, S. N. Taylor, and R. E. Boyatzis, "Antecedents of Organizational Engagement: Exploring Vision, Mood, and Perceived Organizational Support with Emotional Intelligence as a Moderator," *Frontiers in Psychology* 6, article 1322 (2015), doi:10.3389/fpsyg.2014.01322.

19. R. E. Boyatzis, K. Rochford, and K. Cavanagh, "The Role of Emotional and Social Intelligence Competencies in Engineer's Effectiveness and Engagement," *Career Development International* 22, no. 1 (2017): 70–86.

20. J. Gregory and P. Levy, "It's Not Me, It's You: A Multilevel Examination of Variables That Impact Employee Coaching Relationships," *Consulting Psychology Journal: Practice and Research* 63, no. 2 (2011): 67–88.

21. J. Boyce, J. Jackson, and L. Neal, "Building Successful Leadership Coaching Relationships: Examining Impact of Matching Criteria in Leadership Coaching Program," *Journal of Management Development* 29, no. 10 (2010): 914–931.

22. *Andrew Carnegie story:* L. M. Colan, "Coaching: Get It Right the First Time and Avoid Repetition," *Houston Business Journal*, October 12, 2007.

23. Definition from *Merriam-Webster's Collegiate Dictionary*, 11th ed. (Springfield, MA: Merriam-Webster, Inc., 2009).

24. C. Rogers and F. J. Roethlisberger, "Barriers and Gateways to Communication," *Harvard Business Review*, November–December 1991.

25. R. Lee, *The Values of Connection: A Relational Approach to Ethics* (Santa Cruz, CA: Gestalt Press, 2004).

26. H. Reiss, *The Empathy Effect: Seven Neuroscience-Based Keys for Transforming the Way We Live, Love, Work, and Connect across Differences* (Boulder, CO: Sounds True, 2018).

27. Ibid.

28. Adapted from H. Kimsey-House et al., *Co-active Coaching: Changing Business, Transforming Lives* (Boston: Nicholas Brealey Publishing, 2011).

CHAPTER 8

1. Personal communication with Jeff Darner at CRL meeting, November 2–3, 2017.

2. Quotes from statements made in "Coaching in Organizations: Today's Reality and Future Directions," panel discussion at the Thirteenth Annual Leading Edge Consortium conference on coaching, Minneapolis, October 20–21, 2017.

3. Comments from "Coaching in Organizations."

4. Quotation from a magnificent book on peer coaching with a predominant one-to-one focus, P. Parker et al., *Peer Coaching at Work: Principles and Practices* (Stanford, CA: Stanford Business Books, 2018), 2. We also recommend some of the authors' earlier articles: P. Parker et al., "A Relational Communication Approach to Peer Coaching," *Journal of Applied Behavioral Science* 51, no. 2 (2015): 231–252; P. Parker, K. E. Kram, and D. T. Hall, "Peer Coaching: An Untapped Resource for Development," *Organizational Dynamics* 43, no. 2 (2014): 122–129; P. Parker, D. T. Hall, and K. E. Kram, "Peer Coaching: A Relational Process for Accelerating Career Learning," *Academy of Management Learning and Education* 7, no. 4 (2008): 487–503; P. Parker, K. E. Kram, and D. T. Hall, "Exploring Risk Factors in Peer Coaching: A Multilevel Approach," *Journal of Applied Behavioral Science* 49, no. 3 (2012): 361–387.

5. Bill W. *My First 40 Years: An Autobiography by the Cofounder of Alcoholics Anonymous* (Center City, MN: Hazelden, 2000).

6. M. F. R. Kets de Vries, "Leadership Group Coaching in Action: The Zen of Creating High Performance Teams," *Academy of Management Executive* 19, no. 1 (2005): 61–76.

7. See M. Higgins and K. E. Kram, "Reconceptualizing Mentoring at Work: A Developmental Network Perspective," *Academy of Management Review* 26, no. 2 (2001): 264–288.

8. V. U. Druskat and D. C. Kayes, "Learning versus Performance in Short-Term Project Teams," *Small Group Research* 31, no. 3 (2000): 328–353.

9. F. Barrett, *Yes to the Mess: Surprising Leadership Lessons from Jazz* (Boston: Harvard Business Review Press, 2012).

10. Reference in Barrett, *Yes to the Mess*.

11. R. Ballou et al., "Fellowship in Lifelong Learning: An Executive Development Program for Advanced Professionals," *Journal of Management Education* 23, no. 4 (1999): 338–354; and H. Tajfel, "Social Identity and Intergroup Behavior," *Trends and Developments: Social Science Informs* 13, no. 2 (1974): 65–93.

12. Ballou et al., "Fellowship in Lifelong Learning."

13. P. Parker et al., *Peer Coaching: Principles and Practice* (Stanford, CA: Stanford University Press, 2017); see also Parker, Kram, and Hall, "Exploring Risk Factors in Peer Coaching"; Parker, Hall, and Kram, "Peer Coaching: A Relational Process."

14. L. Himelstein and S. Anderson Forest, "Breaking Through," *BusinessWeek*, February 17, 1997, pp. 64–70.

15. One meta-analysis showed that internal coaches helped significantly more on the impact of coaching on desired outcomes than external coaches; see R. Jones, S. Woods, and Y. Guillaume, "The Effectiveness of Workplace Coaching: A Meta-Analysis of Learning and Performance Outcomes from Coaching," *Journal of Occupational and Organizational Psychology* 89 (2015): 249 –277.

16. For competency models of coach certification, see ICFs at https://coachfederation.org/core-competencies; for CCE, see https://careerdevelopmentmusings.wordpress.com/2016/09/06/board-certified-coach-competencies-and-ceuonestop-com-courses-and-webinars-a-crosswalk/; and for WABC, see http://www.wabccoaches.com/includes/popups/competencies.html. For a broader discussion of what should determine a validated competency model, see R. Boyatzis, *The Competent Manager: A Model for Effective Performance* (New York: John Wiley & Sons, 1982); for a thorough discussion of the consequences of credentialing, see J. Fallows, "The Case against Credentialism," *The Atlantic Monthly*, December 1985, 49–67.

17. Personal conversations with Chris Baer, 2017.

18. W. Mahler, "Although Good Coaching Is Basic to Managerial Productivity, Most Organizations Have Difficulty Getting Their Managers to Be Effective Coaches," *Personnel Administration* 27, no. 1 (1964): 28–33.

19. T. E. Maltbia, "High-Impact Performance Coaching: Applying the Four C's Framework to Define, Monitor and Generate Results," *Choice Magazine* 11, no. 1 (2013): 27–32. This segment of the article draws on Mager and Pipe's classic work (R. F. Mager

and P. Pipe, *Analyzing Performance Problems*, 2nd ed. (Belmont, CA: David S. Lake Publishers, 1984).

20. J. J. Dhaling et al. "Does Coaching Matter? A Multilevel Model Linking Managerial Coaching Skill and Frequency to Sales Goal Attainment," *Personnel Psychology* 69, no. 4 (2016): 863–894.

21. P. A. Heslin, D. Vandewalle, and G. P. Latham, "Keen to Help? Managers' Implicit Person Theories and Their Subsequent Employee Coaching," *Personnel Psychology* 59, no. 4 (2006): 871–902.

22. These comments come from two surveys of primary data on millennials: Manpower's 2016 *Millennial Careers: 2020 Vision*, surveying nineteen thousand millennials from twenty-five countries; and American Express/Kantar Futures, *Redefining the C-Suite: Business the Millennial Way*, 2017, which surveyed 1,363 millennials from the US, UK, France, and Germany.

CHAPTER 9

1. Fernández-Aráoz has written extensively on maximizing talent and the process of finding the best people for a position. See his articles in *Harvard Business Review* (C. Fernández-Aráoz, "21st-Century Talent Spotting," June 2014; C. Fernández-Aráoz, B. Groysberg, and N. Nohria "The Definitive Guide to Recruiting in Good Times and Bad," May 2009; C. Fernández-Aráoz, "Hiring without Firing," July–August 1999); and books (C. Fernández-Aráoz, *It's Not the How or the What but the Who: Succeed by Surrounding Yourself with the Best* [Boston: Harvard Business Review Press, 2014]; C. Fernández-Aráoz, *Great People Decisions: Why They Matter So Much, Why They Are So Hard, and How You Can Master Them* [Hoboken, NJ: Wiley, 2007]).

2. B. J. Avolio and S. T. Hannah, "Developmental Readiness: Accelerating Leader Development," *Consulting Psychology Journal: Practice and Research* 60 (2008). 331–347.

3. D. MacKie, "The Effects of Coachee Readiness and Core Self-Evaluations on Leadership Coaching Outcomes: A Controlled Trial," *Coaching: An International Journal of Theory, Research and Practice* 25, no. 2 [2015]): 120–136; and J. Franklin, "Change Readiness in Coaching: Potentiating Client Change," in *Evidence-Based Coaching*, ed. M. J. Cavanagh, A. Grant, and T. Kemp (Queensland: Australian Academic Press, 2005), 193–200.

4. J. O. Prochaska and C. C. DiClemente, "Stages and Processes of Self-Change of Smoking: Toward an Integrative Model of Change," *Journal of Consulting and Clinical Psychology* 51 (1983):

390–395; J. O. Prochaska, C. C. DiClemente, and J. C. Norcross, "In Search of How People Change: Applications to the Addictive Behaviors,"*American Psychologist* 47 (1992): 1102–1114.

5. Viktor Frankl, *Man's Search for Meaning: An Introduction to Logotherapy* (1946; rept. Boston: Beacon Press, 2006).

INDEX

ABOUT THE AUTHORS

RICHARD BOYATZIS is Distinguished University Professor of Case Western Reserve University, Professor in the Departments of Organizational Behavior, Psychology, and Cognitive Science, and HR Horvitz Professor of Family Business at the Weatherhead School of Management, Case Western Reserve University. In addition, he is an adjunct professor in the Department of Human Resources at ESADE Business School in Barcelona. Boyatzis holds a BS in Aeronautics and Astronautics from MIT and an MA and PhD in Social Psychology from Harvard University. Using his well-established Intentional Change Theory (ICT) and complexity theory, he studies sustained, desired change at all levels of human endeavor, from the individual level to teams, organizations, communities, and countries. Since 1967 his research has focused specifically on helping and coaching. Boyatzis was ranked 9th Most Influential International Thinker by *HR Magazine* in 2012 and 2014. He is the author of more than two hundred articles on leadership, emotional and social intelligence competencies, emotional intelligence, competency development, coaching, neuroscience, and management education. His massive open online course (MOOC), Inspiring Leadership Through Emotional Intelligence, has over 780,000 students from 215 countries enrolled through Coursera. His nine books include *The Competent Manager*, the international bestseller *Primal Leadership* (with Daniel Goleman and Annie McKee), and *Resonant Leadership* (with Annie McKee). He is a Fellow of the Association of Psychological Science and the Society of Industrial and Organizational Psychology.

MELVIN SMITH is a professor in the Department of Organizational Behavior and Faculty Director of Executive Education at the Weatherhead School of Management, Case Western Reserve University (with Ellen van Oosten). He is also currently serving as Board Chair of the Graduate School Alliance for Education in Coaching (GSAEC). Smith's research and teaching focus on leadership and emotional intelligence in the workplace, as well as on social exchange relationships, social networks, and the development and use of human and social capital in organizations. His work has been published in outlets such as *Academy of Management Learning & Education*, *Frontiers in Psychology*, the *Journal of Applied Behavioral Science*, *Journal of Management Development*, *Leadership Excellence*, and *Organizational Dynamics*.

Smith is a Board Certified Coach (BCC) and a highly sought-after speaker. He regularly provides training and education services to numerous US organizations in addition to working with executives in Canada, Dubai, India, New Zealand, Scotland, Spain, and Trinidad.

Smith received his PhD in Organizational Behavior and Human Resource Management from the University of Pittsburgh's Katz Graduate School of Business. He also holds a BS degree in General Management and Accounting from Purdue University and an MBA in Marketing from Clark Atlanta University. Prior to completing his doctoral work at the University of Pittsburgh, he spent over fifteen years in a series of sales/marketing management and organization development positions with several *Fortune* 500 companies, including IBM, Pepsi-Cola, and H. J. Heinz.

ELLEN VAN OOSTEN is an associate professor in the Department of Organizational Behavior and Faculty Director of Executive Education at the Weatherhead School of Management, Case Western Reserve University (with Melvin Smith). She is also Director of the Coaching Research Lab, which she cofounded with Richard Boyatzis and Melvin Smith in 2014 to advance research in the field of coaching. Her research interests include coaching, leadership development, emotional intelligence, and positive change. Van

Oosten has published scholarly and practitioner articles that cover topics such as coaching for change, coaching outcomes, leadership vision, and leadership development in organizations. Her work has been published in *Consulting Psychology Journal: Practice and Research*, *Frontiers in Psychology*, the *Journal of Applied Behavioral Science*, *Journal of Management Development*, *Leadership Excellence*, and *Organizational Dynamics*.

As an instructor, Van Oosten teaches in the MBA, Executive MBA, Masters of Engineering Management, and undergraduate programs at Case Western Reserve and regularly delivers workshops for Executive Education clients. She leads the Weatherhead Coaching Certificate Program and is a highly requested executive coach. She holds both the Board Certified Coach (BCC) and Associate Certified Coach (ACC) designations.

Van Oosten received her PhD in Organizational Behavior and her MBA from the Weatherhead School of Management. She also holds a BS in Electrical Engineering from the University of Dayton. Prior to joining the Weatherhead faculty, she spent eighteen years working with organizations to develop leadership talent and held numerous staff positions at Weatherhead, including Assistant Dean for Executive Education and Managing Director of Custom Programs.